A Shepherd Solicitous
for the Whole Church

A Shepherd Solicitous
for
the Whole Church

Bishop Athanasius Schneider
in Conversation with Dániel Fülep & Others

EDITED BY PETER KWASNIEWSKI

Os Justi
Press

Os Justi Press
P.O. Box 21814
Lincoln, NE 68542
www.osjustipress.com

Send inquiries to
info@osjustipress.com

ISBN 978-1-960711-83-0 (paperback)
ISBN 978-1-960711-84-7 (hardcover)
ISBN 978-1-960711-85-4 (ebook)

Typesetting by Michael Schrauzer
Cover design by Julian Kwasniewski
Photo by Allison Girone

CONTENTS

PREFACE TO THE US EDITION

THE STORY OF THIS VOLUME GOES BACK TO Bishop Athanasius Schneider's first visit to Hungary. In 2016, I invited His Excellency into the heart of Europe, Hungary, also known as *Regnum Marianum*. The highlight of his unforgettable journey was the Sacred Liturgy on *Laetare* Sunday. This was the first time since the Second Vatican Council that a pontifical Mass in the *usus antiquior* was offered in our country. His first visit to Hungary gave rise to a book entitled *Regnum Eucharisticum*, including an interview, famous at the time, that was subsequently translated into eight languages.

My trip to Kazakhstan took place in July 2018 at the kind invitation of Bishop Athanasius. During the few days available to us, I was able to talk to him several times. Despite its modest size, this volume's significance lies in the continued relevance of the lessons it contains, which have certainly not lost any of their relevance in the intervening years. Particularly valuable is the account of His Excellency's book *Dominus Est*, from which we learn of the direct influence it exercised on Pope Benedict XVI. The volume helps us to recall the major ecclesiastical events of recent times so that we can better understand the road to the catastrophic multi-year Synod on Synodality. The leitmotif of the volume — "*Exsurge, Domine!*" — is an even more urgent plea today than in the past.

It may be of interest to American readers that the name of the American continent itself refers to the first name of Prince St Imre — *Emericus, Americus* — the only son (and one who died at a tragically young age in 1031) of King St Stephen of the royal house of Árpád, who ruled from 1000 to 1038. Anastasio Vespucci, who was secretary of the

Senate of Florence, most probably gave his son the first name *Amerigo* under the influence of the *cultus* of Prince St Imre in medieval Italy. St Stephen himself, founder of the Catholic Kingdom of Hungary in the year 1000 — the first canonized king in the history of the Catholic Church — offered the Holy Crown of Hungary or *Sacra Corona* to the Virgin Mary after Imre died. Since then, the Virgin Mary has been our Queen and we have been Mary's Land, *Regnum Marianum*.

I express here my thanks to Dr. Peter A. Kwasniewski for publishing a newly edited, definitive version of the interview. The original book was called *Catholic Church, Where Are You Heading?*; the title has been changed for the American edition, with an allusion to an important passage from *Lumen Gentium* no. 23 that says "each [individual bishop], as a member of the episcopal college and legitimate successor of the apostles, is *obliged by Christ's institution and command to be solicitous for the whole Church*, and this solicitude, though it is not exercised by an act of jurisdiction, contributes greatly to the advantage of the universal Church."

The text has been reorganized topically for ease of reading, and six additional interviews have been added as Part 2, further enriching the discourse.

Dániel Fülep
Budapest, January 15, 2024
S. Pauli Primi Eremitae et Confessoris

PART 1

A Conversation with Dániel Fülep

TRANSLATED BY GÁBOR SALLAI

His Excellency Athanasius Schneider, Auxiliary Bishop of the Archdiocese of Saint Mary in Astana, with theologian Dániel Fülep Astana, Kazakhstan, July 2018

INTRODUCTION

"MASTER, DO YOU NOT CARE? WE ARE PERishing!" (Mk 4:38), said the disciples as, in alarm, they woke Jesus sleeping in the boat tossed about by huge waves on Lake Genesareth.

The Catholic Church is facing difficult and extraordinary times. If ever, now is the time to declare that, according to the Catholic faith, not even a pope is entitled to spark a revolution. This dramatic situation, however, is still largely ignored or not taken seriously enough by Catholics. This is partly due to the mainstream Catholic media concealing obvious problems. Painful details are simply left out. Reality is whitewashed or rewritten. It is not only that anomalies are glossed over or even promoted, but false doctrines are propagated, with the secular media gladly joining in. The world exults over any departure from tradition, any step toward secularization, any doctrines changed and "modernized." It is also true that many Catholics lack sufficient knowledge or — what is even worse — do not care about their faith. Modernist religion is subjectivist, emotionalist, separating faith and reason, ultimately leading to agnosticism, which reduces the truths and demands of faith to subjective feelings and to the world's current ideology. That's why the predominance of the heresy of modernism is largely ignored, although symptoms of the crisis of the Church manifest themselves even in the most remote parish.

Many Catholics, and not a few priests and bishops, are indifferent to or even approve of the results of this modernism, and they become appalled if someone tries to get them out of their comfort zone. The faithful are ignorant because of the prevailing silence on the part of cardinals, bishops, and priests. It is only a few critics of the present pope and, in contrast, those who practice "papolatry," defending evidently erroneous decisions of the current pope at all costs, who voice their opinions.[1] There are various reasons for the silence. Some warmly welcome the "change of paradigm"; others are quiet or confused due to insufficient knowledge or information, or are personally interested in protecting their careers or positions; still others are at a loss, tortured by the obvious contradictions. All in all, the faithful listening to sermons or receiving pastoral care are hardly ever presented with the reality, so they are not duly motivated to pray, fast, and do penance for their own sins and those of the world. Thus abandoned, Catholics are like sheep without a shepherd, and they will understandably rejoice to find a bishop, whether from the USA, Guinea, or Kazakhstan, who provides them with authentic Catholic guidance.

To help readers better understand the questions put to Bishop Schneider during our conversation, I believe it will be advantageous if I first present the current state of affairs in the Church.

The Vicar of Christ on earth can be judged by no one but God. Formally, a pope can be corrected only by himself or by his successor.[2] The content of his teaching, however, can be

---

1   It was none other than Father Thomas Rosica, English-language assistant to the Holy See Press Office, who said: "Pope Francis breaks Catholic traditions whenever he wants because he is 'free from disordered attachments.' Our Church has indeed entered a new phase: with the advent of this first Jesuit pope, it is openly ruled by an individual rather than by the authority of Scripture alone or even its own dictates of tradition plus Scripture." Once these words went viral, they were scrubbed off of Zenit. See https://catholicherald.co.uk/vatican-advisor-pope-breaks-catholic-traditions-whenever-he-wants/.

2   Formal correction by the cardinals can be nothing more than an emphatic indication for the pope that there is every indication that he has made erroneous or ambiguous statements. Erroneous or ambiguous papal teaching must be formally corrected by the pope himself, though some have disputed this point: see John Lamont and Claudio Pierantoni, eds., *Defending the Faith Against Present Heresies: Letters and Statements Addressed to Pope Francis, the Cardinals, and the Bishops with a Collection of Related Articles and Interviews* (Waterloo, ON: Arouca Press, n.d. [2021]) and "Call for the Resignation of Pope Francis," *Rorate Caeli*, May 2, 2024.

objectively assessed, and he can freely be asked questions by anybody. False doctrine must be called false doctrine and, as such, it must be dismissed. And if the pope proves to be a tyrant rather than a guardian of faith, if the pope and the papal office come into conflict with each other, if pastoral care is separated from doctrine, and relativism and situation ethics gain ground, we must step forward and act.

Pope Francis calls all people "children of God" irrespective of justification and baptism, thereby distorting the true meaning of faith, love, and peace; he suggests the equivalence of all religions;[3] he gave his approval to a practice which admits divorced and civilly remarried people (that is, adulterers) to Holy Communion.[4] He redefined the ritual of foot-washing on Holy Thursday,[5] spoke highly of Luther and his intentions,[6] approved of the reception of Holy Communion by Protestant spouses of Catholics,[7] changed the

---

3   One example of this is Pope Francis's video message of January 2016 with its syncretistic approach that is incompatible with the *Catechism* and is very much like Masonic doctrines.

4   According to the formal interpretation, Pope Francis' Apostolic Exhortation *Amoris Laetitia* has opened the way for the divorced and civilly remarried to receive Holy Communion without an obligation to practice sexual abstinence. The concession offered by some episcopal norms of application of *AL* constitutes sacrilege against the three sacraments of marriage, confession, and the Holy Eucharist.

5   Pope Francis seems to have developed his own practice of washing the feet of men and women on Holy Thursday, including not only Catholics but also Hindus and Muslims. This practice is against the liturgical norms issued by the pope himself on January 6, 2016. In this way Pope Francis significantly modified the theological meaning of the washing of the feet, breaking its close relationship with the institution of holy orders and the apostolic mission.

6   Pope Francis said that "the intentions of Martin Luther were not mistaken" but "perhaps some methods were not correct." Martin Luther "was a reformer," who "made a medicine for the Church." The Vatican issued a commemorative stamp featuring the excommunicated Luther kneeling together with Melanchthon at the foot of the Cross, and the Holy See called him "a witness to the gospel." Pope Francis calls the Lutheran communities "churches."

7   Ten of the dioceses in Germany are formally authorized by their bishops to administer Holy Communion to the Protestant spouses of Catholics. The initiative by Cardinal Marx and the German Bishops' Conference was approved by Pope Francis in person.

teaching of the *Catechism* in a way that directly contradicts Tradition,[8] and tolerates homosexual propaganda.[9] Moreover, he refuses to provide unequivocal answers to doctrinal questions posed by cardinals, bishops, priests, and laymen.[10] This list of anomalies, which is by no means exhaustive,[11] illustrates the serious crisis we now face.

It is important to note that the pope bears a primary but not an exclusive responsibility for this situation. The current papacy is not a stand-alone phenomenon but has grown out

---

8   On August 2, 2018, Pope Francis ordered the *Catechism of the Catholic Church* to be revised, in no. 2267 on capital punishment. The modified point directly contradicts the perennial teaching of the Church, which declares the death penalty morally acceptable under specific conditions as a way to protect the community. The modification bears significance not only on account of its subject matter but also as a precedent.

9   Several persons who openly propagate the homosexual lifestyle were appointed by Pope Francis to high offices. The Pontiff makes false and ambiguous statements about homosexuality. At Christmas 2017, the Vatican's Christmas Nativity scene on St. Peter's Square included homoerotic statues; some cardinals and bishops openly endorse the blessing of homosexual relationships [a point made much clearer in *Fiducia Supplicans—Ed.*]; the World Meeting of Families 2018 included LGBT propaganda; and there is the scandal around Cardinal McCarrick, as thirty American bishops, including Cardinal DiNardo, president of the bishops' conference, requested clarification of Pope Francis' role in his regard.

10   Pope Francis will not enter into dialogue with the main critics of *Amoris Laetitia*. For years he has refused to answer the questions posed on September 19, 2016 (the *Dubia*) by Cardinals Walter Brandmüller, Raymond Burke, Carlo Caffarra† and Joachim Meisner†. Neither does he respond to the Filial Correction issued on September 23, 2017 (*Correctio Filialis*) or the Kazakhstan Bishops' Statement of December 31, 2017. The Dubia Cardinals also requested an audience, which was not granted by Pope Francis.

11   Pope Francis acts strangely in political terms, too: he often points out the rights of migrants, refugees, and immigrants as well as the obligation to welcome them, but he seems to be ignorant of the consequences of the flood of illegal immigrants and the impossibility of integrating Muslims. The pope does not raise public awareness of the threat of illegal immigration, the Islamic invasion of Europe, the obligations of migrants (e.g., respect for the law), or the right of the target countries to defend themselves. All in all, when it comes to defending ourselves against illegal and aggressive immigration and the alarming Islamic invasion, the pope cannot be counted on. Clearly, his rhetoric favors politicians of the liberal left, who enjoy quoting him on immigration.

of an ongoing crisis—that is to say, the problem is even greater and deeper than it may appear to be at first sight. And as the enemy is already embedded in the highest circles of the hierarchy, the current situation requires unflinching self-defense by faithful Catholics. We must be clear that "the wickedness and snares of the devil"[12] aim to rob us of our eternal salvation.

First and foremost, this must make us even more determined to live a holy life with a special focus on prayer, fasting, and doing penance for the sins committed by ourselves and by others.[13] Faced with the current trials, all of us will soon reach a crossroads, when we must choose to adhere steadfastly to the entire deposit of faith (*depositum fidei*) and avoid being deceived by manipulations and false teaching. Thus, not only must we pray and receive the sacraments, we also need the sound teaching, guidance, and exhortation of good bishops. That is why I decided to visit Bishop Athanasius Schneider and asked him again[14] to clarify the current state of the Church and the world by answering questions extremely relevant to our times.

In his Excellency's presence and listening to his words, I am filled with hope and certitude that the Lord Jesus is always with us in the boat of the Church, even as He was once with the disciples on the stormy lake. Being close to the Lord, we will always be safe because He is the absolute master over the stormy sea of history. Jesus Christ is the supreme and eternal Head of the Church, who has the

---

1 2   *"Nequitiam et insidias diaboli"*: from the invocation of Saint Michael added by Leo XIII to the Prayers after Low Mass.

1 3   Cf. Mk 9:28: "This is the kind that can be driven out only by prayer and fasting."

1 4   I first interviewed Bishop Schneider in March 2016, when—accepting my invitation—Bishop Schneider visited Hungary. For the bishop's presentations, his homily at the Pontifical Mass on Laetare Sunday, and my exclusive interview with him, see the Hungarian and English language book entitled *Regnum Eucharisticum* (ebook version at http://mek.oszk.hu/15500/15547/15547.pdf).

power to rescue us from calamities that, in human terms, are beyond our control. "The Lord Jesus got up and calmed the storm. Then he said to the disciples, 'Why are you so frightened? Have you still no faith?'" (Mk 4:40).

May every reader of this interview be filled with the strength, clarity, and courage provided by the wise, true, and pure words of his Excellency Bishop Athanasius Schneider.

Dániel Fülep
Budapest, August 21, 2018
Revised April 4, 2023

1

Holy Communion—
"It Is the Lord!"

Your Excellency, thank you for your gracious invitation to the Archdiocese of Astana. Allow me to ask you for guidance and instructions regarding a number of timely questions. Dominus Est — It is the Lord!,[1] a famous book by your Excellency, is a great martyrologic and patristic witness on behalf of receiving Holy Communion on the tongue and kneeling as the most worthy gesture before this immense gift. Few know that you took the manuscript of the book to the synod on the Eucharist in 2005,[2] in which you participated as an auditor, and that it had a direct impact on Pope Benedict XVI.

[Bishop Schneider:] During the Synod of Bishops on the Eucharist in 2005, where I participated as an auditor, they discussed the manner of receiving Holy Communion, and also the problematic mode of receiving Holy Communion directly in the hand; the so-called "communion in the

---

1   The Bishop's book *Dominus Est — It Is the Lord!* was published in the spring of 2008 in Italian by the publishing house of the Holy See (Libreria Editrice Vaticana, 2008) and was soon translated into English, German, Estonian, Lithuanian, Polish, Hungarian, and Chinese.

2   The Year of the Eucharist announced by Pope John Paul II was opened by the 48th International Eucharistic Congress in Guadalajara, Mexico on October 10-17, 2004. The Year of the Eucharist was closed by the Eleventh General Synod of Bishops on October 2-29, 2005. The theme of the synod was chosen by Pope John Paul II: "The Eucharist is the source and summit of the life and vocation of the Church." Following the synod, Pope Benedict XVI issued an apostolic exhortation entitled *Sacramentum Caritatis*, summarizing the reflections and recommendations formulated by the synod of bishops, including a wide range of documents from *Lineamenta* [Outline] to *Propositiones* [Recommendations], taking into consideration the *Instrumentum laboris* [Working Document], *Relationes ante et post disceptationem* [Reports before and after the debate], the comments of Synod Fathers, observers, and lay delegates, to determine some basic directions in which new Eucharistic initiatives and zeal are to be promoted in the Church.

hand."[3] In 2005, I prepared my future book *Dominus Est* as
a manuscript. I had a short audience with the Holy Father,
Pope Benedict, during the synod, and I expressed to him
my concern about the situation created by communion in
the hand. The pope answered me that already other bishops
had spoken to him about this problem. I said to him: "Holy
Father, I prepared a manuscript for a book about this topic.
Would you like to have it and to read it?" He answered me:
"Yes, please give it to me." However, I had forgotten to bring
the text with me to this audience. And so I said to the Holy
Father: "I apologize, I forgot the text." The pope said: "There
is no problem. You can give the text to my secretary tomorrow."
It was providential that I had forgotten it, because in the evening I could still write an accompanying letter. In this letter
I expressed a specific request to the pope: "Most Holy Father,
I beseech you in the name of Jesus Christ, please, yourself
no longer give Communion in the hand, but make it so that
when people come to you to receive Holy Communion from
your hands, they will receive it only kneeling and on the
tongue."[4] Then the next day I gave the secretary the text of
my future book and the accompanying letter.

What impact did the book have on Pope Benedict?

After a couple of weeks I got a letter, on the envelope was
written: "Confidential and personal." When I read this on
the envelope, I suddenly felt in my soul that it was the pope's
answer to my letter. When I opened the letter, I read these

---

3 The general modern practice of receiving Communion in the hand is
related to the Lord's Supper of the Calvinists, who deny the Real Presence.
[See Peter Kwasniewski, "Debunking the myth that today's Communion in
the hand revives an ancient custom," *LifeSiteNews*, November 26, 2019. — *Ed.*]
4 Even today, the general rule is that the faithful shall receive Holy Communion on the tongue and kneeling: see *Redemptionis Sacramentum* 90. Administering Communion in the hand is an "indult" or concession granted by
Pope Paul VI under the conditions specified by the Holy See: see *Memoriale
Domini*, the Instruction on the Manner of Administering Holy Communion,
Congregation for Divine Worship, May 29, 1969 (*AAS* 61 [1969]: 541–47).

words of Benedict XVI: "Your arguments are convincing. But as you know, there are powerful groups in the Church who resist what you have asked me to do." He only described the situation and gave me his blessing. Honestly speaking, I did not believe that the pope would do what I asked him to do. Then I published my book *Dominus Est* some years later in the Vatican publishing house in the beginning of 2008, first in Italian. A few months later, on the feast of Corpus Christi in 2008,[5] Pope Benedict XVI did what I had asked him to do. He did this until the end of his pontificate. Since that day, Pope Benedict XVI distributed Holy Communion exclusively in that manner: people had to kneel on a kneeler and receive the Host directly on the tongue. I did not believe that he would do this. When some days later I saw some pictures on a liturgical website, I could not believe it, I was so happy. There was a commentary below saying that from this moment on, Pope Benedict will distribute Holy Communion in this manner.[6] I was so happy that I suddenly knelt down beside my computer and prayed the *Te Deum*.

Some weeks later, I was in Rome and participated in the general audience, and at the end of the audience I approached Pope Benedict and greeted him with the words: "Most Holy Father, may God reward you because of the miracle that happened on the feast of Corpus Christi." He knew what I was speaking about and said to me: "Yes, this mode of giving

---

5   Thursday, May 22, 2008.

6   At a Pontifical Mass in Leuca during his visit to Apulia on June 14–15, 2008, Pope Benedict XVI administered Communion only on the tongue of the kneeling faithful. From that day on the Holy Father set a good example of distributing Communion in the most worthy manner. In an interview of June 25, 2008 to the newspaper *L'Osservatore Romano*, Master of Papal Ceremonies, Msgr. Guido Marini, said that from then on the faithful would have to receive Holy Communion on the tongue and kneeling at papal Masses as the general rule, which had often been the case before: "It is to be noted that, in legal terms, administering communion in the hand is still subject to special permission, which has been granted only to bishops of some bishops' conferences. The procedure of the Pope is aimed to highlight the legal force of the general rule to be applied in the whole Church."

Holy Communion kneeling and on the tongue is more appropriate."[7] It was for me really a deep spiritual joy. I had this deep spiritual joy not because of my ideas, but because of the Lord Himself. He has the right to be guarded in the Sacrament, to be adored, to be respected even in the external manner in which He is received — kneeling and on the tongue.

Can we say that it is because of Dominus Est *that Pope Benedict committed himself to a general rule of administering Holy Communion in this way, as a model for everyone to follow?*

I don't know directly, but at least there was some connection. I don't know if he did this because of my letter or because there were other people who had also asked him to do it this way. In any case it was for me a deep joy.

The synod of 2005 on the Eucharist was attended by Protestant observers, too.[8] Your Excellency had a painfully memorable meeting with a Lutheran "bishop" from Norway.

I had my place close to the ecumenical delegation, and there was a Lutheran bishop from Norway. At the coffee break, I spoke with him, and asked him about the manner in which the Lutherans receive Holy Communion. He answered me that maybe until ten years ago almost all received Holy Communion kneeling and on the tongue, but nowadays the rite is different. I asked him how they changed the rite of Communion. He answered me: "Now we receive Communion

---

7   Cardinal Joseph Ratzinger says: "Holy Communion will only attain its real richness if it is sustained and surrounded by adoration" (*Der Geist der Liturgie: Eine Einführung*, Freiburg 2002, p. 78). In the Apostolic Exhortation *Sacramentum Caritatis*, Pope Benedict XVI states with regard to the reception of Holy Communion: "Receiving the Eucharist means adoring him whom we receive" (no. 66).

8   That second synod of the new millennium was attended by 256 Synod Fathers from 118 countries of the world, including 55 cardinals, 8 patriarchs, 82 archbishops, 123 bishops, 36 presidents of bishops' conferences, and 12 religious brothers and sisters, as well as 12 representatives of the Eastern Catholic Churches.

standing and in the hand." I asked him why they changed
the rite. He answered, saying literally: "Because of the influence of our Catholic brothers."

*As is known, Protestant spouses of the Catholic faithful may receive
Holy Communion "under certain conditions" in accordance with a
document issued on June 27, 2018 by the German Bishops' Conference headed by Cardinal Reinhard Marx. The scandalous decision was
approved by Pope Francis in person. By July 12, 2018, intercommunion
with Protestant spouses of the Catholic faithful had been introduced
in ten dioceses of Germany. Without listing all the dogmatic, patristic,
or canonical counterarguments, let me ask one question only. Is the
following canon of the Council of Trent still in effect: "If any one saith,
that faith alone is a sufficient preparation for receiving the sacrament
of the most holy Eucharist; let him be anathema"[9]?*

It is always valid because this is an infallible decision
of the Church. But the practical observance of this canon
is unfortunately not realized. The majority of the German
bishops started a new movement to allow Protestant people
to receive Holy Communion in some cases. But these few
cases will soon be a general rule. We do not have to be naïve;
they *will* be a general case. Through this action the Church
authorities sin against the sanctity of Eucharist. There is
a general attack against the sanctity of the Eucharist, and
the Eucharist is the heart of the Catholic Church and the
highest expression of the perfect spiritual union of the members of the Church. When you receive Holy Communion
what is required essentially is the full faith, not only in the
Eucharist but in *all* Catholic truths. The Eucharist is the
synthesis of all good and of all truth in the Church. One
cannot say: "It is sufficient that they believe in the Eucharistic presence." They have to believe in *all* Catholic dogmas,
otherwise the reception of the Eucharist will represent a lie.

---

9   Council of Trent, Session 13, Can. 11.

The Holy Eucharist is the highest expression of the unity of the members of the Church — a unity in doctrine and in submission to the shepherds of the Catholic Church. Eucharistic Communion expresses and realizes the perfect union of the members of the Church. When Church authorities admit Protestants to Holy Communion, saying "you can receive Holy Communion while remaining Protestant or Orthodox," they commit an official public lie regarding the true meaning of the Church and of the Holy Eucharist. This also propagates the indifferentism and relativism that consist in viewing Catholic truth and the Protestant and Orthodox beliefs as more or less equivalent.

2

Sacred Liturgy and the Priesthood

Communities practicing traditional liturgy often ask the question how both Latin and the vernacular can be used properly at the same Mass. I think the best solution is to have the readings of the Mass and the Propers in the vernacular, too, with some of the church hymns also in the native language. What do you think of this?

In the transcript of the debates that took place during the Second Vatican Council, one can read that almost all the Council Fathers asked that it be possible for the readings of the Mass to be proclaimed directly in the vernacular; even Archbishop Marcel Lefebvre favored this. The readings belong to the part of the Mass called the "Mass of the Catechumens." Even though the entire liturgy of the Mass and all its parts have glorifying and adoring God as their first aim, in this first part the Word of God in the readings is addressed to the ears and the understanding of the faithful. A worthy and solemn proclamation of the readings in the vernacular would not diminish the sacredness of the liturgy of the Mass, as long as the rest continued to be celebrated in Latin. At international gatherings, all the readings should be proclaimed, of course, in Latin.

Celebrating liturgy and participating in it fruitfully require due preparation on the part of the priest and the faithful alike. Modern practice risks being negligent and unworthy, while the danger of the traditional practice is an aestheticism for its own sake with a liturgy "too beautiful," aimed at perfection at the expense of the spirit. How is this danger to be correctly managed?

The true Catholic principle is the synthesis of exterior and interior — of exterior beauty and perfection with interior participation. These two aspects should not be separated and should not be played off one against the other. The exterior aspect proclaims the greatness of God, the author of all beauty, and helps to foster the interior participation. We have always to be vigilant to avoid any theatricality and self-centeredness in the execution of the rites and music during the sacred liturgy.

Some communities tend to admit only highly qualified musicians to the scholae cantorum *and use Latin exclusively, sometimes dropping the simplified Gregorian chant in the vernacular and Hungarian church hymns altogether. Certainly, the deeply spiritual Latin is the mother tongue of the Church, but how is elitism to be avoided so that liturgy can be easily approached by the simple faithful, too?*

We have to say, first, that liturgical music in Latin provided by highly competent musicians is spiritually beneficial for the simple faithful too, because it lifts their souls to heaven, to God, Who is essentially a mystery. On the other hand, the simple faithful also like to praise God with their own voices and in their mother tongue. In my opinion, in a Latin *Missa cantata* held in parishes, worthy hymns in the vernacular could also be sung — for example, during the entrance and during the departure of the celebrant. The same could sometimes be done during the Offertory and Holy Communion after the Propers have been sung in Latin. The presence of truly worthy hymns in the vernacular would not diminish the sacredness of the liturgy. On special occasions — for instance, in Solemn Pontifical Masses — the music could be done entirely in Latin.

Conservative priests still face difficulties when they want to celebrate Mass ad orientem. *Despite all arguments to the contrary, celebration versus populum[1] is still considered by most bishops and priests to be a binding law "introduced by the Council." Sadly enough, most of the sanctuaries erected and consecrated, even to our day, are completely*

---

1   *Versus populum* (towards the people) is the modern liturgical stance in which the priest offers the Mass facing the people.

unusable for ad orientem liturgy.[2] *What's more, traditional liturgical spaces are still being destroyed in the name of modernization. Cardinal Sarah, who spoke up for Mass ad orientem in 2016, was silenced by the pope himself.*[3] *What can be done in such a situation?*

We should try to spread the theological, historical, and pastoral arguments in favor of *ad orientem* celebration. There are many good studies and comments about this topic (Cardinal Joseph Ratzinger, Cardinal Robert Sarah, Father Uwe Michael Lang, Father Stefan Heid, etc.). We should lay claim to the right of the faithful to *ad orientem* celebration. We should try to achieve *ad orientem* celebration wherever and whenever possible.

Valid and legitimate ordination of priests and bishops is vital for the Church. The validity of the new ordination rites introduced by Pope Paul VI is of primary importance. Leo XIII judged the Anglican rite invalid because their rite of ordination does not explicitly refer to all the major elements of ordination.[4] *This is embarrassing because the same omissions seem to have been made in the new Catholic practice of ordination, too.*[5] *How are the new ordination rites to be assessed?*

---

2   *Ad orientem* (to the east) is a phrase commonly used to describe a particular orientation of a priest in Catholic liturgy, with priest and people looking in the same direction. Although in its origins it is connected with the east where the sun rises, subsequently the phrase was at times detached from geographical direction and concerned more with a single linear direction toward the apse of the church building. The earliest known use of the exact Latin phrase *ad orientem* to describe the Christian practice of facing east when praying is in Augustine's *De Sermone Domini in Monte*, probably of AD 393. Two centuries earlier, Tertullian in his *Apologeticus* (AD 197) used the equivalent phrase *ad orientis regionem* (to the region of the east) to indicate the practice.

3   Edward Pentin, "Father Lombardi: Cardinal Sarah's *Ad Orientem* Suggestion 'Misinterpreted,'" *National Catholic Register*, July 11, 2016, www.ncregister.com/blog/edward-pentin/father-lombardi-cardinal-sarahs-ad-orientem-suggestion-misinterpreted.

4   "The sacraments of the New Law, as sensible and efficient signs of invisible grace, ought both to signify the grace which they effect, and effect the grace which they signify" (DH 3315; cf. 3316–3319).

5   The former rite of ordination clearly reflected the Church's teaching that priesthood is based on the offering of the Eucharistic sacrifice and includes

Pope Paul VI changed the sacramental form only of the episcopal consecration. The sacramental form of the priestly and diaconal ordination remained the same. To administer a sacrament validly, what is necessary is valid matter, valid form, and the intention to do what the Church does. In the case of the episcopal ordination, Paul VI took the sacramental form from the Byzantine Rite. The popes always through history recognized the validity of the Byzantine episcopal consecration. I don't see a *doctrinal* problem in the sacramental form of episcopal ordination introduced by Paul VI. The same pope also took the sacramental form of the sacrament of Confirmation from the Byzantine rite; and the Catholic Church has always recognized the validity of Confirmation in the Byzantine church. Hence, the theory that says the new rite of episcopal ordination is invalid is without foundation and is not serious.

Pope Leo XIII said that Anglican ordinations are invalid because they are incomplete, that is, the very essence of priesthood is not referred to explicitly. The main parts of the new ordination rites seem to be less clear than formerly. Isn't there a fatal similarity between the Anglican ordination rite and that introduced by Paul VI?

It is not similar at all. The new rite of episcopal ordination is completely Catholic. The Anglicans, in contrast, adapted the rite of episcopal ordination to their Protestant theology, with no mention of the Eucharistic sacrifice and of the sacrificing priesthood. Therefore, their ordination is surely invalid, because of the objective defect of the right intention. In the case of the reform of the ordination rites made by Paul VI, there are sufficient references to the doctrine of the Catholic priesthood and the true sacrifice of the Eucharist.

---

the power to forgive sins. In his encyclical *Ad Catholici Sacerdotii*, Pope Pius XI still confirms explicitly: "Primarily, the priest's power lies in consecration, offering the Eucharistic sacrifice and dispensing the Blood and Body of Christ, secondarily in forgiving sins and proclaiming the Word of God." In the new rite these powers appear at best vaguely: the priest is seen as a presbyter rather than a *sacerdos*.

Cardinal Christoph Schönborn has clarified his views on female ordination, saying that women priests would be "too profound a change." However, he signaled his support for the introduction of deaconesses.[6] *Shortly afterwards, cardinal-designate Luis Ladaria, Prefect of the Congregation for the Doctrine of the Faith, wrote a strongly-worded article in Vatican newspaper L'Osservatore Romano, saying that the prohibition on women being ordained to the priesthood is "definitive."*[7] *Archbishop Luis Ladaria cites the writings of Pope John Paul II, who taught in* Ordinatio Sacerdotalis *that the Church cannot ordain women, as well as the current Pontiff, who in* Evangelii Gaudium *confirmed the male-only priesthood. This teaching, the CDF prefect said, is "a truth belonging to the deposit of faith." How is it that one who was editorial secretary for the 1992* Catechism of the Catholic Church *does not understand that this question is not open for discussion?*

It is very sad that a cardinal of the Church speaks ultimately against the definitive truth of the Church, which Pope John Paul II stated, namely that the Church has no competency to allow female ordinations. This doctrine is definitive and unchanging, declared John Paul II. A cardinal may not pronounce publicly his doubt about this doctrinal statement of John Paul II. Such a cardinal contradicts the constant teaching of the Church when he says the issue could be

---

6   In an interview with Austrian news site OE24, the Archbishop of Vienna said that while there were female deacons in the early Church, he did not foresee a female priesthood in the future. "Ordination [of women] is a question that surely can only be settled by a Council," he told *Die Presse*. "A pope cannot decide this by himself. This is too large a question for it to be settled from the desk of a pope." "Kardinal Schönborn im Oster-Interview: Ein Konzil für die Rolle der Frau," *Salzburger Nachrichten*, March 31, 2018, www.sn.at/politik/innenpolitik/kardinal-schoenborn-im-oster-interview-ein-konzil-fuer-die-rolle-der-frau-26058967. "Cardinal Schönborn: women priests 'too profound a change' for the Church," *Catholic Herald*, June 20, 2018, www.catholicherald.co.uk/news/2018/06/20/cardinal-schonborn-women-priests-too-profound-a-change-for-the-church/.

7   See "CDF prefect confirms: ordination of women is impossible, teaching is permanent," *Catholic World News*, May 29, 2018, www.catholicculture.org/news/headlines/index.cfm?storyid=37098.

discussed again. It cannot be discussed. John Paul II referred only to the priestly ordination, and inclusively of course to the episcopal ordination, but did not mention the diaconal ordination. The truth of the sacrament of ordination says that there is only one sacrament of ordination, not three sacraments of ordination. The Second Vatican Council stated that the diaconate is part of the sacrament of Holy Orders: it is a sacramental reality.

Therefore, the diaconate, being a part of the sacrament, cannot be conferred on women, even as the other two parts of the sacrament, i.e., the presbyteral and episcopal ordinations, cannot be conferred on women. You cannot give one part to women, and not the two other parts. It would be a contradiction of the meaning of the sacrament of ordination itself. From this point of view, it is also theologically impossible to ordain women deacons. We have sufficient proofs and documents from Church history about so-called female deacons in the ancient Church. They had a special prayer for ordination, not the same as for men. The Church was aware that it is not the same. The ancient formulas of the ordination of deaconesses were not sacramental, they were similar to the formulas of the consecration of virgins or of abbesses in the Roman Pontifical. In some rare cases, mostly in the Oriental churches, the deaconesses could approach the altar or take the Holy Sacrament. Today also women can go during Mass to the tabernacle and to the altar and take the Holy Sacrament and distribute it to the faithful, even without being ordained a deaconess, and without even being an instituted acolyte. There is, therefore, nothing surprising when, in ancient times, deaconesses could in some cases touch the Holy Sacrament or the altar.

However, even in the Oriental churches they never proclaimed the gospel during the Eucharistic Sacrifice. In the Latin Church, Carthusian nuns had the custom of proclaiming the gospel in Matins, in the Divine Office — not, however, during Mass. The prioress of the Carthusians could wear the maniple and the stole. This was the only exception in the Latin Church. However, this is not a convincing argument in favor of a female diaconate. There was no prayer of ordination for these Carthusian nuns, and it was not a general use in the Church. The Latin Church has never had deaconesses. When something in the Church is established by divine right, it must be—and be witnessed to—always and everywhere. So it was with the male deacons, priests, and bishops: they existed always and everywhere. This is a clear sign of divine institution. The prayers for the ordination of a deacon and the institution of a deaconess were substantially different, and the office of deaconesses was not everywhere and always, but only in a limited time and in particular places.

It is important to note that current terminology for the sacraments is the result of a centuries-long process. The term "deaconess" is clearly found in some documents of the early Church, but it refers to women who assisted in baptizing other women or attending female patients and never entailed altar service or ordination.

Of course there are plenty of documents; we do not have to enter into these details. I would only expand on the terminological aspect. In Gallia (now France), in the sixth to eighth centuries there was a custom of calling the wife of a deacon *diacona*. However, she was not ordained; she was spoken of in this way only because she was the wife of the deacon. The wife of a priest was called *presbytera*, and the wife of a bishop was called *episcopa*. In the first millennium, married men were ordained to priesthood or episcopacy in the Latin Church; they were, however, obliged to live in perfect continence from the moment of their ordination. Hence, this local custom from Gallia is not a precedent for the ordination of female priests or bishops.

This year [2018] a "Synod on Youth" will be celebrated...

It is very sad that the working document for the Synod on Youth uses the propaganda language of "LGBT." We should not use this expression in a Church document in a positive or even in a neutral way. The apparently neutral use of the expression LGBT in that document is a sign that the Catholic Church has to be open and to accept the so-called LGBT people and their lifestyle. These people live against the commandments of God, they practice homosexuality and thereby destroy their own dignity. They put themselves in danger of eternal damnation. It is a very sad phenomenon that the propagandists of homosexuality are now using the upcoming synod as a tool to promote gender ideology and the legitimization of homosexual activity. That also happened in the two family synods. There were evident manipulations inside the synod leadership. There is thus a foundation for assuming that there could be similar tactics and methods of manipulation in the upcoming synod. The goal is to promote moral relativism in the Church and the positive acceptance of homosexuality.

Next year will behold the so-called Pan-Amazonian Synod, which will have the theme: "Amazonia: New Paths for the Church and for an Integral Ecology." This is the theme chosen by Pope Francis for the synod of bishops dealing with the region of Amazonia that will take place in Rome in October 2019. The preparatory council of the synod has 18 members including Cardinal Claudio Hummes, bishop emeritus of São Paulo, president of the Pan-Amazonian Ecclesial Network, and Bishop Emeritus Erwin Kräutler, who led the Brazilian diocese of Xingu from 1981 to 2015. Both men are known to promote the ordination of tested married men ("viri probati") in the Latin Church, so that is also expected to be on the agenda of the Pan-Amazonian Synod.

The goal and trend of this synod are already clearly manifested in several statements of the bishops and cardinals appointed as its participants. They speak openly about the issue of celibacy. They say that it will be examined, and that there should be the option of ordaining married men to the priesthood. They call these men *viri probati*. One can fear that they will use the next synod to promote this idea, and ultimately to abolish celibacy, using cunning formulations—for instance, limiting the *viri probati* to "exceptional cases" and to "special regions." It is clear to everybody that there would be a domino effect in the entire Church, and one can foresee this; we don't have to be naive. Unless God intervenes next year, the abolition of the apostolic rule of priestly continence and celibacy will probably happen. Therefore, we have to join all our prayers and efforts in praying and imploring God that He may not permit a pope to approve such proposals, which would ultimately and practically abolish priestly celibacy in the entire Church.

You often hear even bishops saying that the law of celibacy is nothing but a technical legal means of preventing problems of succession, dating back to the Middle Ages. The truth is, however, that priestly celibacy is already prescribed by the Synod of Elvira in circa 300 AD.[8] *It is primarily based on the teaching of the apostle Paul,*[9] *the way of life of the apostles after Pentecost, Christ's call,*[10] *and the life of our Lord Jesus totally dedicated to the Father. Following Christ with all one's being is the very heart and purpose of priestly celibacy. Essentially, it is supernatural, thus it is always confronted with incomprehension and attacked by the enemies of the Church.*

This is clear. The oldest document, which reminds the clergy to observe the traditional law of priestly continence, was issued by the Council of Elvira in Spain at the beginning of the fourth century. The traditional norm said that bishops,

---

8   "Bishops, presbyters, and deacons, and all other clerics having a position in the ministry, are ordered to abstain completely from their wives and not to have children. Whoever, in fact, does this shall be expelled from the dignity of the clerical state" (Canon 33).

9   See 1 Cor 7:7, 32–34.

10   Mt 12:19; 19:12.

priests, and deacons could live with their wives, albeit observing sexual continence. This was the meaning of celibacy in ancient times. The continence required then and now is always the same. St. Cyril of Jerusalem, for example, affirmed in 380 in one of his catecheses that a good priest should not have conjugal relations with his wife. Most of the priests in those times still had wives. Note his strong expression: a "*good* priest" has no sexual relationships with his wife. In the time of St Augustine, in 390, there was a synod in Carthage which reminded the clergy to observe perpetual sexual continence, saying that this is an apostolic tradition. Surely, the Church in the fourth century had better knowledge of what was an apostolic tradition than we do today!

The Roman Church always kept this apostolic tradition. Only the Greek Church at the end of the seventh century abandoned the apostolic law of perfect continence and allowed deacons and priests to have sexual relations with their wives; however, this was not allowed to the bishops. We see here a contradiction. Why could bishops not have conjugal relations with their wives? When later Oriental churches were united with Rome, Rome made an exception or in some way granted an indult for them in order to facilitate their conversion, since the main concerns were doctrinal issues about the Holy Spirit and papal primacy. The Oriental churches accepted the main dogmatic determinations, and the Holy See, in order to facilitate the union, said you may continue your law from the seventh century that priests and deacons can have conjugal relations with their wives.

In that law of the Greek Church from the seventh century, we see another contradiction. The first contradiction was the episcopacy. The second contradiction is that when a wife of a priest or of a deacon dies, he cannot marry again. Why not? When the law accepts the compatibility of being a priest and having sexual relations with a wife, why can it not accommodate a new wife after the priest has become a widower? I see no logic here. The only logic is the contradiction of apostolic tradition. Moreover, if a celibate man is ordained deacon and priest, he cannot marry at all; this remains valid in the Orthodox Church. It shows that the treatment of celibacy in the Orthodox Church is full of incongruities.

Theology professor Stanley Jaki[11] remarked that a profound theological relationship between celibacy and the priesthood manifests itself even in the church discipline of the Byzantine Church: the married priest cannot sleep with his wife the night before offering the Eucharistic sacrifice.

The Orthodox priest cannot offer the Eucharist when the night before he had conjugal relations with his wife. To licitly celebrate the Holy Eucharist, the priest has to be sexually continent. However, a priest is always an *alter Christus*, another Christ, every day of his life. Usually a Catholic priest celebrates Holy Mass every day, and this is another reason why he has to live in perpetual sexual continence.

A priest's sexual activity (even if he is validly married) and the offering of the Eucharistic sacrifice are ultimately incompatible?

Yes. Why does he observe sexual continence only the night before, but when he has had relations with his wife four days before, he can offer the Liturgy? Is there so much difference between these situations? This is a contradiction as well.

Removing the law and theology of celibacy affects the essence of the priesthood. As a grave consequence, the Church will be weakened. Through his wife and family, for whom schooling, doctors, peace, and financial security must be provided, the priest will necessarily be more

---

11   Stanley L. Jaki (Szaniszló László Jáki, 1924–2009) was a Hungarian Catholic priest of the Benedictine Order, theologian, physicist, professor of the history and philosophy of science, and recipient of the Templeton Prize. He was author of over fifty books, including *Theology of Priestly Celibacy* (Christendom Press, 2004).

dependent on the state or on the Church bureaucracy. In times of persecution or oppression, a married priest can be easily blackmailed or silenced. Unfortunately, the history of the Orthodox Church and Communism offers many such examples.

Yes, there was collaboration with Communism. It is evident that those Orthodox priests who have a family and children will often, out of a natural instinct to protect their spouse and children, collaborate, when necessary, with the government. This is understandable. In some cases, to be fair, these pastors or Orthodox priests were also martyrs. However, the majority of martyred priests during the persecution were priests who lived in celibacy. It is easier for a celibate priest to resist the government or to resist an unjust and unchristian policy even to the point of being persecuted and put to death. Yet this is only one factor. The *main* factor is human fear, which a celibate priest can also have! And there were also some collaborators amongst the celibate priests. Because of careerism, many priests in our days, too, are collaborators with the unchristian political powers. Today we have no small number of clerics and bishops who, because of careerism, collaborate with the new dictatorship — the gender ideology dictatorship. They collaborate for the sake of promotion in Church offices. This is a human weakness. We have to develop, therefore, the spirit of militancy for Christ. We have to be true soldiers of Christ. We must develop this spirituality again.

3

Modernism

Pope John XXIII said that "All evils have one source: the ignorance of truth."[1] Unfortunately, there are not many people who really know the figure of John XXIII, who is praised almost exclusively for his act of calling the last Council. Many of his teachings have largely been "forgotten."[2] To understand the Second Vatican Council correctly, should we perhaps start by getting acquainted with the movers and shakers of it — the popes, the prominent bishops, the theologians?

The intention of Pope John XXIII in convoking the Council was primarily pastoral in character. Hence, he did not intend that the Council would make final doctrinal statements or bring a final solution to theological discussions (such as, for instance, the theme of episcopal collegiality). The Council had to explain Catholic truths in a way that would be better understood by unbelievers of our time, yet, in so doing, avoid any doctrinal ambiguity. Unfortunately, a group of liberal-minded bishops and theologians, supporters of a doctrinal relativism — that is, of the modernism that was condemned by Pius X — gained such influence that they took over the strategic positions in the commissions and also in the leadership structures of the Council. Ralph Wiltgen's *The Rhine Flows into the Tiber* and Roberto de Mattei's *The Second Vatican Council — An Unwritten Story* offer plentiful documentary proofs of this.

The truly Catholic protagonists of the Council were to be found in the minority that gathered under the banner of the *Coetus Patrum Internationalis*. This was organized mostly thanks to the efforts of two Archbishops: Geraldo Sigaud of

---

1 Pope John XXIII, encyclical *Ad Petri Cathedram*, June 29, 1959, nos. 1–2.
2 As is, for example, John XXIII's Apostolic Constitution *Veterum Sapientia* on the Latin language (February 22, 1962).

Brazil and Archbishop Marcel Lefebvre of France. Thanks to this courageous minority, many dangerous and ambiguous doctrinal formulations in the texts of the Council were corrected, which explains why they were able to receive such clear majority votes. The most important bishops and theologians at the Council were the ones who courageously fought for the clarity and integrity of Catholic truths in the Council's texts and for the maintenance of continuity with the constant doctrinal, liturgical, and disciplinary practice of the Church.

It remains an enigma how John XXIII and Paul VI could promote to key positions in the Council's leadership structures and commissions those ecclesiastics — bishops, cardinals, theologians — who were known sympathizers with a modernist and relativistic theology.

What led to the separation of faith and practice?

The separation of practice from doctrine started, in my opinion, with the *"ralliement,"* the obligation imposed by Leo XIII on all French Catholics to accept the radical anticlerical French government. Seventy years later, John XXIII again took up this idea and realized it through the program of the Second Vatican Council. John XXIII said that immutable doctrine is one thing, while the explanations of doctrine and its practical applications are another, and the latter should be adapted to modern times. This is true in principle. However, a *separation* between doctrine and practice was developed after the Council to such an extent that now obvious contradictions between perennial doctrine and daily practice in the life of the Church are undeniable. This in my opinion is not a good approach because, since the time of Jesus Christ Our Lord and the Apostles, the Church always believed that practice has to conform to doctrine, *always*. If a given praxis weakens the doctrine, that praxis has to be corrected.

4

Invalid Papal Elections?

On February 15, 1559, Pope Paul IV[1] issued a Papal Bull entitled Cum Ex Apostolatus Officio, codifying the explicit invalidity of any papal election where the man ascending to the throne of St Peter has fallen into heresy or committed the sin of schism or become alienated from the Church, even if only once or temporarily—saying this provision "shall be valid for all times." Those abandoning the Catholic faith, the apostates and the schismatics, must be deprived of office and suffer other severe punishments, too, while their supporters must be eo ipso excommunicated. Clearly, Paul IV aimed to protect partly the hierarchy, especially the papal office, from Protestant heterodoxy, partly the faithful from corruption and eternal damnation.[2] This Bull has never been withdrawn. Moreover, some of its elements appear even in the latest papal and canonical provisions.[3] How is this document to be interpreted correctly in light of the current state of the Church?

There are some disciplinary norms and papal bulls that were not explicitly revoked but whose norms are nevertheless no longer valid in the Church. It is not always necessary to revoke a norm explicitly. Through time and new

---

1 Gian Pietro Carafa (1476–1559) became successor of Marcellus II under the name of Pope Paul IV. Despite his old age, he was determined to fight for reforms (the elimination of abuses) and against the spread of Protestantism and its infiltration into the Church throughout his papacy, 1555–1559.

2 "The abomination of desolation, which was spoken of by Daniel the prophet as he was standing in the holy place, should never reach Us; desiring, as much as possible with God to do what We can, for the sake of Our Pastoral duty, to seize the foxes, who sow destruction in the vineyard of the Lord, and to keep the wolves at a distance from the sheepfold, lest We seem mute dogs, unable to bark, and be destroyed with the evil farmer or like the hireling." Source: www.todayscatholicworld.com/cum-ex-apostolatus-officio.pdf.

3 Cf. John Paul II, *Universi Dominici Gregis, AAS* 88 (1996): 305–43; CIC 332, 1024, 1025, 1031, etc.

laws, the older laws become obsolete and no longer valid. I have not studied this papal bull carefully. According to the Code of Canon Law, a candidate for the papacy must be a baptized Catholic man.[4] Even a layperson could be elected, he's not required to be a priest or a bishop or a cardinal. The basic requirement is to be a Catholic — and that means, not a heretic. The candidate for the papacy has to be Catholic, he cannot be half-Catholic or one-third-Catholic. He has to be a full Catholic, a man who professes the entire Catholic faith.

In a television interview on September 23, 2013, Cardinal Godfried Danneels, Archbishop Emeritus of Mechelen-Brussels, admitted that he had been part of a secretive group within the Church that wanted to remove Pope Benedict XVI. "The group wanted Bergoglio to immediately follow Karol Wojtyła as the head of the Church." The cardinal says that the St. Gallen mafia[5] did exist from 1996 to 2006, and in 2013 it became active again. As per a 1996 provision by John Paul II, any organizing or consultation activity influencing papal elections entails excommunication,[6] which is also true for any secret negotiation on the election of the successor.[7] What if Cardinal Bergoglio was part of this group?

---

4   Cf. CIC 332, 1024, 1025.
5   Cardinal Danneels says: "The Sankt-Gallen group is a sort of posh name. But in reality we said of ourselves, and of that group: 'The Mafia.'" There is abundant information about this group in Julia Meloni's book *The St. Gallen Mafia: Exposing the Secret Reformist Group within the Church* (Gastonia, NC: TAN Books, 2021). Among the alleged members of this secretive group were Belgian Cardinal Godfried Danneels, Dutch bishop Adriaan Van Luyn, Cardinal Walter Kasper and Cardinal Karl Lehmann from Germany, Cardinal Achille Silvestrini of Italy, and British Cardinal Cormac Murphy-O'Connor.
6   "The Cardinal electors shall further abstain from any form of pact, agreement, promise or other commitment of any kind which could oblige them to give or deny their vote to a person or persons. If this were in fact done, even under oath, I decree that such a commitment shall be null and void and that no one shall be bound to observe it; and I hereby impose the penalty of excommunication *latae sententiae* upon those who violate this prohibition." *Universi Dominici Gregis*, no. 81.
7   *Universi Dominici Gregis*, no. 79.

To my knowledge, in ancient times even an excommunicated cardinal had the right to vote. The excommunication itself was not an impediment to vote, and to be voted for — because canon law requires only that the candidate be a man, baptized, and Catholic. In my opinion, if these cardinals, who made a pre-conclave machination, did incur automatic excommunication, they could still vote; and even if one of them was elected pope, it would not directly affect the validity of the election. There have been many such cases in history, specifically in the Renaissance, or earlier in the so-called *"saeculum obscurum."*[8] Such elections via mafia methods are, of course, rare. For instance, before the election of Alexander VI in the Renaissance time there was propaganda in his favor. Alexander VI[9] even committed the crime of simony — he paid to be elected. However, no one then considered and no one now considers Pope Alexander VI to have been an invalid pope.

The Church has already seen several occasions where popes were elected in doubtful circumstances. However, their election was not subsequently pronounced invalid. This to me is a very wise norm; otherwise, a huge confusion would arise. How can you prove exactly and juridically that there were maneuvers and so on prior to the conclave? And even if we accepted the hypothesis that the election of Pope Francis was invalid because of these alleged machinations, he is *now* nevertheless the true pope. For according to the age-old praxis of the Church, a pope invalidly elected is validated when the entire Church accepts him *de facto* as pope. So it was in the moment when all cardinal electors offered him their obedience first in the Sistine Chapel and

---

8 The *saeculum obscurum* (dark age) was first so named and identified as a period of papal immorality by the Italian cardinal and historian Ceasar Baronius in his *Annales Ecclesiastici* in the sixteenth century. This period in the history of the papacy begins with the installation of Pope Sergius III in 904 and lasts for sixty years until the death of Pope John XII in 964.
9 Pope Alexander VI, born Rodrigo Borgia, was pope from 1492 until 1503.

then publicly during the Mass of his enthronement. They all recognized him publicly as the pope. The entire episcopate and the entire Church names the pope in the Mass. This is a *de facto* acceptance of the pope. In the hypothetical case of an invalid election of Pope Francis, such a general acceptance would be a *de facto* healing of the defects of the election. In such a case, one could speak of a kind of *sanatio in radice.*[10]

This is a very wise tradition of the Church, because it helps to avoid schisms, which the Church has experienced many times. Sometimes there was real anarchy and people did not know who the true pope was. To avoid such anarchy, the more constant tradition of the Church says that, in virtue of a general acceptance of an invalidly elected pope, his possession of office is validated. It is a wise tradition and accords with common sense.

It's been five years since Cardinal Godfried Danneels announced this, but several alarming questions haven't been clarified since. Does membership of this group entail excommunication? Was Cardinal Bergoglio part of this group? Why did Cardinal Danneels speak about it? Was he afraid of something? It is appalling that no one has ever denied the fact and the Holy See and the Cardinals have not issued any official explanation to date.

I hope that in the future, in order to avoid doubts, the tradition that holds that an invalid papal election will be healed by the general acceptance of this pope by the entire Church will be codified in law. In this way everyone will know it. The tradition could be expressed in the Code of Canon Law or in a papal document about the election of the pope.

---

10   A concept from marriage law: "*sanatio in radice*" (healing in the root) is the curing of an invalid marriage in accordance with CIC 1161 § 1 so that marriage may become a recognized sacramental marriage in accordance with the canon law of the Church.

Bishop René Gracida,[11] *among others, believes that the activity of the St. Gallen mafia is canonically illegal under the laws of the 1996 Apostolic Constitution* Universi Dominici Gregis *promulgated by John Paul II. If this is true, the validity of the papal election may be in doubt.*[12]

Such arguments have no foundation, even if this opinion is affirmed by one or more bishops. The truth is not based on who speaks and how many speak; one has to examine the common tradition of the Church concerning an alleged invalid papal election.

---

11   Bishop René Henry Gracida (b. 1923), Emeritus of Corpus Christi, Texas, USA.

12   Bishop Gracida asserts this at his blog "abyssum.org"; he has published many articles arguing that Francis is an antipope. According to Gracida, some cardinals, including Jorge Bergoglio, violated canon law by plotting his election and they are therefore now excommunicated.

5

Reactions to *Amoris Laetitia*

On December 31, 2017, the Feast of the Holy Family, in the year of the centenary of the apparitions of Our Lady at Fatima, the Catholic bishops of Kazakhstan published a statement on Amoris Laetitia. *Your Excellency invited all bishops to declare publicly their support or issue a similar text.[1] As far as I know, only ten signatures were collected.[2]*

I had been in contact with some bishops who would not sign the statement but who, nevertheless, agreed with its content. For various reasons, they could not give their name publicly.

I know two Hungarian bishops who have reservations about Amoris Laetitia *but will reveal them only confidentially, if at all. There must be many more like them. The Church has 5,507 bishops at present.[3] It is impossible that, out of the whole College of Bishops, there are only ten signatories of the Kazakhstan statement. We can also see that Pope Francis doesn't even like questions and punishes anybody who speaks up for traditional teaching. Is this great silence due to fear?*

---

1   In conversation with *LifeSiteNews* on January 15, 2018, the auxiliary bishop of Astana, Kazakhstan, said that all of the world's bishops who have an email address in the *Annuario Pontificio* were sent the text of the profession via email. "It is up to each bishop to declare publicly his support or to issue a similar text," Bishop Schneider said. "The public reaction of Cardinal Eijk from Utrecht could be a first example of this kind." Source: Diane Montagna, "Bishop Schneider invites world's prelates to sign Profession of Immutable Truths," *LifeSiteNews*, January 30, 2018, www.lifesitenews.com/news/exclusive-athanasius-schneider-invites-worlds-bishops-to-sign-profession-of.

2   Archbishop Tomash Peta, Archbishop Emeritus Jan Paweł Lenga, and Auxiliary Bishop Athanasius Schneider; in addition, Cardinal Emeritus Janis Pujats, Archbishop Emeritus Carlo Maria Viganò, Archbishop Emeritus Luigi Negri, Bishop Emeritus Andreas Laun, Bishop Emeritus Elmar Fischer, Bishop Emeritus René Henry Gracida; Auxiliary Bishop Marian Eleganti.

3   Source: www.catholic-hierarchy.org/bishop/ll.html. (As of May 1, 2024, the number is 5,779. — *Ed.*)

Yes, many bishops are afraid. In the introduction of our Statement we expressed regret for the fact that there are now several sets of norms for the application of AL, at different levels of the hierarchy, that permit Holy Communion for the divorced who have attempted a second marriage, and that unfortunately some of these norms received the approval of the supreme authority of the Church. Our Statement appeared as an implicit criticism of Pope Francis, who approved the norms of the bishops of the region of Buenos Aires.[4] Some bishops were afraid to sign the Statement because they did not want to be labeled critics of the pope. I think even if we had not included those words about the supreme authority of the Church, certain bishops would still not have had the courage to sign, because, according to the general opinion, such an act would be viewed as a criticism of the pope.

These bishops are afraid of being labeled as the pope's critics, even in the slightest way. In my opinion, this is *not* an authentic position for a bishop, who is a doctor of faith by divine law, and not only by the Church's law. The bishops are not employees of the pope, they are also brothers of the pope. A brother must be able to speak to the pope when his own conscience says to him that there is something that damages the integrity of the faith in the behavior of the pope — when he tolerates an abuse that contradicts the constant teaching and the constant practice of the Church in a very important issue — for example, the sacraments, the indissolubility of marriage, the holiness of the Eucharist. In such cases, a bishop should speak openly — of course in

---

4   Pope Francis declared that his private letter of September 5, 2016 to the delegate of the Buenos Aires region of the Argentine Bishops' Conference and the regional bishops' interpretation of *Amoris Laetitia* are "part of the Church's magisterium" (*AAS* 108 [2016] 1071–1074). Hence, there is no doubt that Pope Francis's Apostolic Exhortation *Amoris Laetitia* opened the way for the divorced and civilly remarried to receive Holy Communion without practicing sexual abstinence.

a respectful way, even asking the pope to correct the abuse, which, in this case, the pope unfortunately himself supports. I think that such behavior of bishops towards the pope should be considered normal. Unfortunately, we do not yet have this climate in the Church.

I hope that in the future a norm will be incorporated into the Code of Canon Law stating that, in exceptional cases, when a pope by his words, his deeds, or his omissions in some way contradicts the constant teaching of the Church or weakens it, the bishops have not only the right, but the duty to make an admonition to the pope, a respectful, fraternal admonition, either privately or, when necessary, even publicly. I believe this should be stated in the future as a norm in the Code of Canon Law. Such a canonical norm will change the entire atmosphere in the Church. This will benefit the entire Church and be an effective help for the pope too, so that he will not do things that cause confusion in doctrine and in sacramental practice. The canon should be framed, of course, very carefully, and limited only to doctrinal issues or to the sacramental praxis that has always been observed in the entire Church.

Cardinal Raymond Burke, Cardinal Walter Brandmüller, Cardinal Joseph Zen and Your Excellency were key speakers at a conference in Rome on April 7, 2018. The conference Catholic Church: Where are you heading? *adopted a declaration highlighting the "contradictory interpretations" of* Amoris Laetitia, *Pope Francis's apostolic exhortation on the family, and the confusion over doctrine and pastoral practice that has ensued.[5] The conference drew great attention worldwide. How do you assess the atmosphere of the meeting?*

---

5   The conference, organized by Friends of Cardinal Carlo Caffarra, was one of the last wishes of the archbishop emeritus of Bologna, who died September 6, 2017. Source: Edward Pentin, "Conference on Confusion in the Church: Final Declaration," *National Catholic Register*, April 7, 2018, www.ncregister.com/blog/edward-pentin/declaration-of-faith-released-defending-church-teaching.

The atmosphere was very positive. Unexpectedly, a great number of people participated. There were no more seats in the conference hall! I heard that there were more than 400 people. It was a familial atmosphere, in which all members were aware of the common danger. This was for me a gathering of a family, from the little ones to the old ones; all had a sense of responsibility and concern about the current situation in the Church. At the same time, it was a joyful atmosphere, because the majority were lay people, and they realized that they are not abandoned by the shepherds, because of the two cardinals who were present, Cardinal Brandmüller and Cardinal Burke, and myself, a bishop. Cardinal Zen joined the conference via a recorded speech. There was an atmosphere, on the one hand, of consolation and of joy and of family, and on the other hand, an awareness of the great confusion that currently reigns in the Church. These good and simple people were thirsty for clarity in doctrine. This was my impression.

The first speaker of the conference was Cardinal Brandmüller, focusing on the correct interpretation of the sensus fidei *(sense of the faith) on the part of the faithful, in connection with John Henry Newman's 1859 essay* On Consulting the Faithful in Matters of Doctrine. *Amidst the current doctrinal confusion, that is an issue of great relevance. What is the main lesson to be learned from Newman's teaching?*

In the main part of his statements, Cardinal Brandmüller quoted Cardinal Newman, who had researched the situation of the Church in the fourth century, during the giant Arian crisis. Cardinal Newman formulated a conclusion that became famous: in the fourth century the Catholic faith was saved more by the "*ecclesia docta*" than by the "*ecclesia docens*,"[6] in other words, the faith was preserved more by the simple faithful than by the hierarchy. Cardinal Brandmüller expanded

---

6 *Ecclesia docta* — the Church taught; *Ecclesia docens* — the teaching Church.

on this thought of Newman's by clarifying that in matters of faith there is no "majority vote." Even if only a numerical minority has the true faith, this minority constitutes the true majority since it preserves the immutable faith of all times. Cardinal Brandmüller said that matters of faith cannot be submitted to some referendum or to media polls. We must be careful to remain independent of the media's opinions and other forms of pressure. As I remember, these were the main points of the statement of Cardinal Brandmüller.

In an interview[7] of August 14, 2017 in the Catholic newspaper The Wanderer, *Cardinal Raymond Burke confirmed that some of the teachings of Pope Francis "must be" formally "corrected." As yet, however, this has not been realized and Cardinal Burke did not even refer to it at the conference.*

I think we have to see the goal of a formal correction of the pope. Until now, different appeals have been made to the pope. Before the celebration of the Synod on the Family in 2015, there was an appeal to the pope from around one million people from all over the world. They asked the pope not to change the immutable doctrine and praxis of the Church concerning divorced people. Together with Archbishop Tomasz Peta and Archbishop Jan Paweł Lenga I made a public appeal at the beginning of 2017 with a prayer that the pope would clarify the issue of the admittance of divorced and civilly remarried people to Holy Communion. This indeed is the core issue of *Amoris Laetitia*. Then we made a public profession of the truth on December 31, 2017. And there are still the *dubia* of the four Cardinals,[8] which have not yet been

---

7   Don Fier, "Interview with Cardinal Burke (Part 2): Discriminating Mercy: Defending Christ and His Church with True Love," August 14, 2017, http://thewandererpress.com/catholic/news/frontpage/interview-with-cardinal-burke-discriminating-mercy-defending-christ-and-his-church-with-true-love-2/.
8   In a letter of September 19, 2016, Cardinals Walter Brandmüller, Raymond L. Burke, Carlo Caffarra, and Joachim Meisner sought from Pope Francis an official and public clarification of the ambiguous statements in

answered. It was known all over the world that the pope had received the text of the *dubia*, yet he did nothing. The situation has become worse in spite of all these appeals; last year the pope officially approved the norms of the bishops of the Buenos Aires region, which foresee "in special cases" the admittance to Holy Communion of unrepentant adulterers.

I think that—humanly speaking—a formal correction will not change the pope's position. What is the meaning of a formal correction? One also has to be realistic and prudent, and ask what is the best way of serving the Church, of helping the faithful. When we can foresee that the correction will not have an effect on the pope, then I think it is meaningless to make a formal correction. On the other side, we, the cardinals and bishops, have to do all we can to strengthen the faithful. Hence, we published several declarations to strengthen the faithful. I see no other possibilities at the moment.

The basic requirement is to pray very intently that God might illuminate the pope. Of course, we can also hold conferences to stress perennial Catholic teaching on these subjects. Maybe we could also prepare and spread a kind of oath against the most dangerous errors of our time. This could be made maybe by a group of theologians, and then shared for all who wish to reaffirm their faith. Then individual bishops can gather their faithful or parish priests in the parishes and publicly profess these Catholic truths. In my opinion, this would be a concrete and efficacious means to address the current doctrinal confusion. The ultimate change comes only when God intervenes, when he illuminates the pope or when He gives us a future holy and courageous pope.

---

the Apostolic Exhortation *Amoris Laetitia* following the two synods on the family. The *Dubia* included five questions, which, however, have not been answered by the pope. "*Dubium*" is a canonical form of petition where the dilemma presented by the petitioner can simply be clarified by saying yes or no. The pope or the relevant congregation is not bound by this one-word form: if they find it more convenient, they can elaborate on their arguments.

Your Excellency gave a talk about "The Apostolic Holy See of Rome as Cathedra Veritatis"—*the Chair of Truth. Would you sum up the main points of your presentation?*

I spoke about the chair or seat of Peter (and thus, of the papacy) as a *cathedra veritatis*, a seat of the truth. The basic divine mission of Peter and his successors consists in proclaiming the truth, in handing on the truth integrally, and in defending the truth. *Cathedra* means a place from which someone officially delivers teaching; this applies above all to the bishops. The pope is the bishop of Rome and the supreme teacher. My idea was to recall what is the basic mission of the pope, of the chair of Rome. It is essentially a chair, a *cathedra*, of truth. I gave examples of the Church Fathers who used similar expressions. Therefore, we have to invoke spiritual help from heaven to protect the pope in his basic duty of proclaiming the truth.

In your presentation you quoted the papal oath. This oath, which was made by many popes during their coronation, hasn't been used for a long time. More recently, since Paul VI, popes have not had a coronation ceremony, haven't worn a tiara,[9] and haven't sworn an oath. To ensure the purity of faith and reinforce the papal office, it would be beneficial to reintroduce the solemn profession of faith by the pope and the papal oath of tenacious adherence to the faith.

---

9   The tiara or triple crown (*triregnum*) is an ancient symbol of power. The triple crown carries manifold symbolism. First, it refers to the fact that the Roman pontiff is "Father of princes and kings, guide of the world, vicar of our Savior Jesus Christ" (*Pontificale Romanum*, 1596). Paul VI stopped wearing the tiara in 1964, selling it on auction for the benefit of the poor. Today it is exhibited in the Basilica of the National Shrine of the Immaculate Conception in Washington, D.C. From then on, the coronation ceremony has been replaced by a "solemn ceremony of the inauguration of a pontificate," where the pope puts on the *pallium*. The coat of arms of Pope Benedict XVI includes only the papal miter or *infula*. The *pallium* and the *infula* as well were originally worn only by the pope and it was only later that the *pallium* became a symbol of every metropolitan archbishop and the *infula* of a bishop, while the specific sovereign authority of the pope was indicated by the triple crown.

Without doubt, it is necessary. Such an oath is not only good, but necessary. This oath of fidelity to Tradition was made by the popes over a long period of time. Reintroducing it would help the faithful and the bishops to be confirmed in the integral Catholic faith. An oath of fidelity to Tradition should also be taken by the bishops. I hope that this papal oath will be codified in the future in Canon Law, so that a newly elected pope will have to make a profession of faith and the oath of fidelity to Tradition in front of the entire Church.

What was the reception of the conference in April and of its final declaration? It seems that it was ignored by the mainstream Catholic press. Did you notice any reaction?

As we discussed earlier, the general climate and atmosphere in the episcopacy and among the cardinals is characterized by intimidation. They are intimidated because they are afraid to be labeled as enemies or critics of Pope Francis; so they are afraid. The career security of these bishops obviously rests on the current administrative staff in the Vatican and also partly on media and public opinion. There is a general atmosphere of fear and intimidation, and hence we could not expect public support or a positive reaction. The faithful laity and simple priests, however, demonstrated good reactions. They wrote letters of gratitude from all over the world. The bishops remained silent. There was a negative reaction from the newspaper of the Italian Bishops' Conference. This newspaper used demagogic expressions, saying that the conference was "a rebellion against Pope Francis." The newspaper used very unfair, demagogic rhetoric. Nevertheless, we have to continue to speak the truth regardless of the reactions we can expect.

6

Our Lady

One characteristic of modern times are the proliferation of Marian apparitions and messages, as if we are more in need than ever of guidance and warning. Consider La Salette. Maximin Giraud and Mélanie Calvat, two young shepherds at La Salette, France, reported that on September 19, 1846, the Blessed Virgin appeared to them and entrusted them with a message.[1] She said that "in the year 1864 Lucifer, together with a large number of demons, will be unloosed from hell;[2] they will put an end to faith little by little, even in those dedicated to God. They will blind them in such a way that unless they are blessed with a special grace, they will take on the spirit of these angels of hell; several religious institutions will lose all faith and will lose many souls.... The Church will witness a frightful crisis.... Rome will lose the faith and become the seat of the Antichrist,"[3] etc. These messages are relevant today.

In your talk at the conference in Rome you quoted the original text of the exorcism written by Pope Leo XIII in 1884, adding that the dramatic sentence "In the Holy Place itself, where the See of Holy Peter and the Chair of Truth has been set up as the light of the world, they have raised the throne of their abominable impiety" was later removed by Pius XI to avoid scandal. Today, however, this clause seems

---

1   On September 19, 1851, Pope Pius IX formally approved the public devotion and prayers to Our Lady of La Salette, referring to its messages as "secrets." On August 24, 1852, Pius IX mentioned the construction of an altar there. The same papal bull granted the foundation of the Association of Our Lady of La Salette, formalized on September 7. On August 21, 1879, Pope Leo XIII formally granted a canonical coronation for the Virgin Mary's image at the Basilica of Our Lady of La Salette. The message of the visionaries focuses on the conversion of all humanity to Christ. St. John Vianney, St. John Bosco, and the writer Joris-Karl Huysmans were all influenced by La Salette.
2   On September 28, 1864, The International Workingmen's Association was founded in London by Karl Marx and Friedrich Engels.
3   Quotations drawn from www.thepopeinred.com/secret.htm.

*to be really prophetic. The current crisis of the Chair of St Peter was
practically predicted by the authentic Marian apparitions at La Salette
and Fatima. How is it that so many, even the popes, fail to see these
signs—with Leo XIII as an exception?*

I think that this part of the message of La Salette is very
important for our times, in view of the confusion due to loss
of faith inside the Church. Pope Leo XIII wrote an exorcism,
a prayer to St. Michael the Archangel. Originally, it was a
longer version, not the short version that we are familiar
with from reciting it after Mass. In the longer version there
is a place where Leo XIII himself states: "in Rome, in this
holy city where the Antichrist established his throne." It is a
mysterious expression. Later this longer version was printed
in an edition of the *Rituale Romanum*, I think at the end
of the nineteenth century. However, in subsequent editions
of the *Rituale Romanum*, under the pontificate of Pius XI,
that phrase was cancelled. Leo XIII's expression about the
throne of the Antichrist in Rome in the prayer of exorcism
is similar to an expression in the secret of La Salette. The
question remains, how should we interpret this expression in
the secret of La Salette and in the prayer of Pope Leo XIII?
Maybe Leo XIII meant the Freemasonic government in Italy
that was established in Rome against the papacy. Note that
the text of the secret of La Salette and of the prayer of Leo
XIII does not say that the throne of the Antichrist will be
in the Vatican, but in Rome.

In any case, I think we should take seriously Our Lady
of La Salette's and Pope Leo XIII's indication that great evil,
and even the Antichrist, will be present in Rome. The presence of evil in Rome penetrates to some extent even into
the Vatican because there is no guarantee that there will
never be infiltrations of anti-Christian powers into the Vatican. In some way, we can say today that there are evidently
some anti-Christian powers operating inside the Vatican. We
can see this manifestly in particular statements and actions

and in various conferences that are organized in the Vatican. There have been conferences where atheists and promoters of abortion and the homosexual ideology were invited by Vatican authorities to speak. These are already clear signs that even inside the Vatican there is an infiltration of anti-Christian powers.

The legacy of Marx, Engels, Lenin, and Stalin still casts a dark shadow over the whole world. Russia has managed to spread its fallacies everywhere because, unfortunately, Russia has not been consecrated to the Immaculate Heart of Mary the way the Blessed Virgin wanted.[4]

I don't know exactly. But one thing is sure: Our Lady of Fatima did not ask for the consecration of the entire world, but only of Russia. I think that an explicit consecration of Russia should be done by the pope, in the form Our Lady asked: by the pope in moral unity with the entire episcopate.[5] I think it should be done, and I believe that there would then flow more graces for humanity. Of course, as you said, Russia is not converted. However, we can see that it is converted partly, because the persecutions stopped, and even the state now, the government supports the Church — the Orthodox Church. One can see revival in the Orthodox Church. We can speak of a partial but not a full conversion, because full conversion means to be converted to the fullness of truth,

---

4   "In August 1941, Sister Lúcia wrote her third memoir in which she described the apparition of July 13, 1917. She said that the Virgin told them: 'God wishes to establish in the world devotion to my Immaculate Heart. If what I say to you is done, many souls will be saved and there will be peace.... I shall come to ask for the consecration of Russia to my Immaculate Heart. If my requests are heeded, Russia will be converted, and there will be peace. If not, she will spread her errors throughout the world, causing wars and persecutions of the Church. The good will be martyred, the Holy Father will have much to suffer, various nations will be annihilated. In the end, my Immaculate Heart will triumph. The Holy Father will consecrate Russia to me, and she will be converted, and a period of peace will be granted to the world.'" Source: www.ewtn.com/library/mary/firstsat.htm.

5   Pope Francis consecrated Russia — together with Ukraine — to the Immaculate Heart of Mary on March 25, 2022. —*Ed.*

and this is the Catholic faith. As long as the Orthodox are not united with Peter, with the pope, they are not in the full truth, therefore there is not yet a full conversion.

The conversion of Russia can only mean its coming back into communion with the only Church of Christ, that is, the Catholic Church.

Exactly. I repeat: to be converted means the full truth. The full truth is to be united with Peter, the pope of Rome.

I wonder what a marvelous role a Catholic Russia could play in the triumph of the Immaculate Heart of Mary based on its impact on Asia and the rest of the Orthodox Church.

I don't know—it is more a speculation. We have no basis to know this exactly. It could be. We can only speak of a possibility. We don't know how God directs history, and history depends on the free will of man, on free collaboration with God. There cannot be a prophecy that has a 100% execution in the future, because factors happen in the future that depend on the free will of the people who act in history. This is an important point. What does the conversion of Russia mean? It is not only to be converted to Christ in some way, but to be converted to the full Catholic faith. We have to insist on this. Such a conversion of the Orthodox Russian Church would without doubt have beneficial consequences for the entire Church and for humanity.

7

Politics and the Church

European Commission president Jean-Claude Juncker opened a series of exhibitions in Karl Marx's hometown of Trier on May 4, 2018. They include a huge bronze statue of Marx donated by China. It was officially unveiled the next day, May 5, the bicentennial of Marx's birth. The sculpture of Marx proves to be somewhat controversial but Jean-Claude Juncker spoke in positive terms about him.[1] China's opinion is understandable, but it is absurd and scandalous that the European Commission president should say that Marx was just a "philosopher" without any heavy responsibility. The first sentence of the Communist Manifesto reads as follows:[2] "A specter is haunting Europe — the specter of communism." Within two generations (1917–1987) communism occupied one third of the world. It was only Christianity and Islam that had spread at such a speed before. Undoubtedly, communism led to atheism, persecution of the Church, apostasy, the suffering and death of one hundred million people worldwide.[3] Your Excellency has had plenty of opportunity to experience communism here in Kazakhstan. The Catholic Church has been an ardent opponent of Marxist ideology from the very beginning. While we see documentaries about Hitler, Nazism, and the persecution of the Jews almost every day, and monuments are erected in commemoration of them everywhere, offenders are called to account, and compensations are paid, the hundred million victims of communism are almost completely forgotten, socialists are

---

1   "Karl Marx was a forward-thinking philosopher with creative aspirations," he said. "Today he stands for things which he is not responsible for and which he didn't have anything to do with, because many of the things he wrote were redrafted to mean just the opposite."
2   *The Communist Manifesto* (originally *Manifesto of the Communist Party*) is an 1848 political pamphlet by Karl Marx and Friedrich Engels.
3   See Stéphane Courtois et al., *The Black Book of Communism: Crimes, Terror, Repression*, trans. Jonathan Murphy and Mark Kramer (Cambridge, MA: Harvard University Press, 1999).

in power almost everywhere in Europe, and the president of the EU erects a huge statue of Marx.

Yes, this behavior of the politicians you mentioned demonstrates to me that in some way they have "outed" themselves. The European Union leadership is, basically, neo-Communist. By these actions they outed themselves. Before, they tried to hide their commitments by changing names, by giving other names to their parties. In my opinion, the European Union is a form of neo-communism and neo-Marxism, which in some ways continues the ideology—a kind of statist ideology—of the former Soviet Union. Now we have a new Soviet Union in the European Union. Marxism is ultimately an ideology against family. In some of their writings, Marx and Engels say that the ultimate goal of communism will be to abolish all differences, even the differences in the family, and consequently the family will be abolished, because, according to Marx, the family is the last bourgeois institution. Now, the European Union is fulfilling and realizing this plan of Marx and Engels that seeks to destroy the family, and the last differences inside the family. We have now the new gender ideology, which destroys family and disfigures human nature. In this we can see the final step of Marxism and neo-communism.

They give themselves a new name. They will be not so naïve as to name themselves neo-Marxists or neo-Communists. They use other names, maybe "New Democrats" and so on. The Communists also liked to call themselves "democrats." China calls itself a "democratic republic," but there is no democracy there at all. The Soviet Union and the Eastern bloc countries always said that they have *true* democracy and that in capitalist countries there was no democracy. I was in school in the Communist period and I still remember that in the fifth grade we had to learn that *true* democracy is found in the Soviet Union, in communism. We are now observing facts and deeds that show how the European Union is a kind of new Soviet Union. We should say this outright in order to unmask them, showing that they are the new face of communism and Marxism.

Is it, then, more than the mere survival of Communism?

I would not say that Communism returned in new clothes, but that there is a further development of Marxism. A further, qualitative development in the degradation of humanity.

The most recent phase of Marxism, which has produced feminism and gender ideology, is just as devastating as the previous one. It attacks life indirectly when it challenges the moral and natural basis of marriage and sexuality and directly when it promotes contraception and abortion. The real disaster, however, is that, distracting you from eternal salvation, it kills your spirit. "Do not be afraid of those who kill the body but cannot kill the soul; fear him rather who can destroy both body and soul in hell" (Mt 10:28).

Yes. The Communists killed people bodily, but they also killed souls with materialism and atheism. The new communism and Marxism of the European Union with gender ideology has spread almost to the entire world. It is directed and orchestrated by world political powers, primarily through the United Nations. This is the case in the United States, too, not only in Europe. It is a common program and basically a Masonic program. Today, they may not kill the citizen bodily, but they do kill his soul in a worse manner than the Communists of the Soviet Union did: they are now perverting the very concept of nature and of the human being. At least in Soviet communism the natural law as to the difference between man and woman was still recognized. In the Soviet period in the Eastern bloc countries and especially in the Soviet Union, homosexuality was unthinkable. Officially it was taught to be against nature. They taught us atheism in school, but they also told us that homosexuality is against nature and is against reason—that it has to be forbidden.

Nowadays the neo-Communists, the neo-Marxists in the world, in the European Union, want to destroy the meaning of nature itself. We are facing now a direct revolt against God. It is more dangerous than the political revolt by the historical Communists.

When thought is separated from truth, words lose their original meaning. The Catholic faithful must beware. To think rightly, the original meaning of words must be restored. For example, the term "revolution" has been used incorrectly in a positive sense since the Reformation and the French Revolution. Theologically, however, revolution means opposing the order established by God. The first revolutionist is Satan himself, who causes opposition against God. Genuine revolutions are always against order, while battles restoring order are counterrevolutions.[4]

Yes, it is very important to state this. Revolution means to change the order established by God. The first revolutionary was Satan, and he inspired all other revolutions. There is a very good book about this idea: *Revolution and Counterrevolution* by Plinio Corrêa de Oliveira.

Yes, I must tell you that my question was directly inspired by this excellent book...

I would recommend reading it. The author gives a very clear, deep, convincing analysis of the concept of revolution throughout human history. I think it would be worthwhile to make Corrêa de Oliveira's book better known.[5]

---

4 In this sense, the Protestant Revolt (1517), the silent revolution of establishing the Grand Lodge of London (1717), the French Revolution (1789-1799), and the October Revolution (1917) were "genuine revolutions" because they waged war against Christ and the Church. However, the Hungarian uprising of 1956, for example, endeavored to overthrow the usurping Communist dictatorship and is therefore to be theologically considered as a *counter*revolution because it aimed to restore the order established by God. Comrades were right to see the events of '56 as theoretically opposed to the Communist revolution of 1917.

5 Originally published as *Revolução e Contra-Revolução* in the Brazilian cultural journal *Catolicismo* in April 1959 (Parts I and II) and in January

By the end of the nineteenth century, the Magisterium of the Church and the bishops seem to be reluctant to specify the exact nature of revolutions.

But they did—the popes, especially Pope Leo XIII, and other popes till the Second Vatican Council. They spoke very clearly about the meaning of revolution and its evils.

What I meant is that the same Pope Leo XIII already supports the idea of a republic explicitly.[6] The project of a republic is also revolutionary, since it opposes hierarchy and monarchy. Human demands take the place of the divine laws as the main point of reference. According to the principle of the sovereignty of the peoples' rule, which arises in the Enlightenment, the authority of a state and its government is created and sustained by the consent of its people, who are the source of all political power. How is this to be reconciled with Catholic faith and truth?

Well, it was more a prudential political decision of the pope than a spiritual or theological decision. He wanted to have peace with the French government in those times, at the end of the nineteenth century. The government was very anticlerical, very Masonic. There was a resistance among the political and social Catholic bloc against this radically anti-Christian French government. The Catholics were mostly organized as monarchists, they had no real alternative. Unfortunately, the French Masonic government put so much pressure on the pope that he yielded. In my opinion, it was a mistake on the pope's part—the so-called "*ralliement*," when the pope ordered French Catholics to accept, in obedience, the current structure of the French republic and its government. In my opinion, that was an abuse of papal power. A pope cannot give commands in areas that

---

1977 (Part III). English translation: *Revolution and Counter-Revolution* (Spring Grove, PA: The American Society for the Defense of Tradition, Family and Property, 1993).
6   Leo XIII, Encyclical *Au Milieu des Sollicitudes*, February 16, 1892.

do not belong to his mission. Christ gave him authority to command the faithful to obey in matters of faith and morals, not in matters that are neutral and belong to the social aspect of public life. He is the teacher of faith first. Of course, he can pronounce on social problems, but not to the extent of ordering people in contingent social and political affairs. The majority of French Catholics in those times were monarchists, and this was entirely legitimate. The same pope had already taught that one can be a monarchist or a republican. Of course, there could be also a Catholic republic . . .

Assuming that people believe in God, obey Christ and the Church, and the state takes the divine law as a starting point.

The radical Masonic and anticlerical French government of those times weakened the validity of the divine law and Catholic Faith in society. After the *ralliement* ordered by the pope, the united social political bloc of Catholics started to fragment. This unfortunately weakened the political power of French Catholicism very much. Thus, we see the error in the political decision of Pope Leo XIII. In theory, this pope was very strong and clear in doctrine, and he even issued an encyclical against Freemasonry, against all the errors of his time. His are very precious encyclicals; we have to state this. On a practical level, however, Leo XIII in some way already supported the separation of practice from doctrine.

Today Freemasonry is largely considered a ridiculous conspiracy theory with no major impact,[7] although its specific symbols and ideology often

---

7 The faithful do not take the menace of Freemasonry seriously in part because for some time even the Church has kept quiet about it. After it was banned for centuries, the new Code of Canon Law does not even refer to it overtly. Even worse, Church members maintain open relations with Freemasonry; for example, the day after Pope Francis was elected, the Grand Orient of Italy issued a solemn declaration, congratulating him and expressing its great expectations. Emblematic notions originating in Freemasonry are now

come up in the world and the Church. Not only does Christ have fol-
lowers, the devil has them too. Alongside the city of God there is the
city of the devil. Wheat and cockle grow together. We Catholics have
to take far more seriously that the powers of darkness have spawned
real and effective worldly structures.

Freemasonry is quite organized in different social and political networks, and it is naïve to deny this. It is against the evidence. Freemasonry is a powerful organization all over the world. In order to deceive the people, Freemasons say that they exist only to do humanitarian work. Through such a tactic of deceit, they can work more effectively with their anti-Christian plan; and they do it. Their tactic is to infiltrate organizations and even the Church, rather than to fight directly and frontally against them. Their tactic, their military tactic, is to infiltrate. In a war it is really more intelligent to infiltrate the enemies than to fight them directly. It is a more efficient and intelligent tactic. The Freemasons do this, because they have the prudence of the flesh, and not of God.

Historically, in the nineteenth century and in other times as well, there were priests and bishops who confessed themselves members of Freemasonry. In other cases, there were very clear indications that a priest or a bishop belonged to Freemasonry. In our time, we cannot deny the fact that there

---

often used by the Holy See itself. Freemasonry was explicitly banned by Clement XII, Benedict XIV, Leo XII, Gregory XVI, Pius IX and Leo XIII [see Peter Kwasniewski, "Freemasonry and Catholicism: Implacable Enemies," *The Remnant*, July 22, 2020, https://remnantnewspaper.com/web/index.php/fetzen-fliegen/item/4987-freemasonry-and-the-catholicism-implacable-enemies — *Ed.*]. As per can. 2335 in the 1917 CIC ("*Nomen dantes sectae massonicae aliisve eiusdem generis associationibus quae contra Ecclesiam vel legitimas civiles potestates machinantur, contrahunt ipso facto excommunicationem Sedi Apostolicae simpliciter reservatam*"), Catholics associated with Freemasonry or similar organizations were automatically, i.e., *latae sententia*, excommunicated, which could be lifted only by the Apostolic See. The 1983 CIC, however, does not mention Freemasonry; thus, excommunication lapsed pursuant to can. 6 § 1 and § 3. Nevertheless, the Congregation for the Doctrine of the Faith issued a declaration on November 26, 1983 confirming that Freemasonry is irreconcilable with true faith and reinforced the ban thereon.

exist secret clerical groups or cliques that are in some way linked to Freemasonry and receive orders from its leadership. Such clerical cliques linked to Freemasonry, even if they formally do not belong to it, have a hidden power in the Church, specifically to promote their candidates to high ecclesiastical positions (episcopate, cardinalate) and in order to have more influence in that way. This is the prudence of the flesh, and Our Lord said that the children of darkness, the children of the world, are more prudent than the children of the light. Such clerical cliques or networks mask themselves with a variety of names, so that, when asked if they are Freemasons, they can say "No" without directly lying. Even though they may have another name for their group, they have the same spirit of Freemasonry — that of naturalism, together with doctrinal and moral relativism. There are today cardinals, bishops, and priests who advocate naturalism and who make the main concern of the Church's work the care of earthly and temporal realities. When the same clerics promote relativism, saying that all religions are in some way equal and all are going the same way, they are advocating clear Masonic ideas. When the same clerics promote the acceptance of homosexuality and of gender ideology, they are achieving a clear Masonic agenda. In our time even bishops or cardinals are members of important Freemasonic lodges, which helped them in their ecclesiastical career, which give them their ideological orders, and which provide them with worldly honors and pleasures. Some of these clerics, when they open their mouth, start to speak a typical Masonic language, or in a Masonic spirit at least.

The problem with Freemasonry is that it is so cunningly secret that you cannot have documentary proofs for all their members. No one has access to their personal files; they will not give anyone access to these archives. We can only guess with a high likelihood that a particular person is a member of Freemasonry. Some of the Freemasons, even some politicians, sometimes confess publicly that they are members of Freemasonry. They can do this when the Freemasonic authority gives them permission to do it, or because they have nothing to lose.

We, Hungarians, who live in the Carpathian Basin in the middle of Europe, have firsthand experience of the profound impact of Freemasonry's ideas on international politics mainly in connection with the institutions of the European Union. Freemasonry significantly influences not only the USA but also the EU, firmly controlling legislation and sanctioning policy. By destroying faith, morality, and nature it wants to transform society fully.

I think it is useful for me to speak about Freemasonry, because its adherents are the operators working behind the scenes to de-Christianize Europe and to spread naturalism, relativism, and even the new gender ideology. In France, for instance, some known Freemasons confess publicly that they are promoting abortion, gender ideology, and the new migration policy. It would be important and useful to speak about the real and concrete aims of Freemasonry and to warn people — including Catholics — away from entering a Masonic organization. It would be good to expose the principal ideas of Freemasonry. Then people will see and say: "Ah, this is very similar to what is now going on inside the life of the Church. There is a predominant influence of naturalism, of doctrinal and moral relativism, and of anthropocentrism. These are the ideological pillars of Freemasonry, at whose center stands man and not God." These three aspects of anthropocentrism, naturalism, and relativism prominently characterize the life of the Church since the Second Vatican Council.

Some wonder if Freemasonry is worth dealing with; they may find it too complex or hidden to assess. Is it useful for us to identify and name ill-intentioned secret societies and other evil mechanisms in the world?

Yes, we have to do this, because in our days we see how Freemasons and their sympathizers inside the Church openly state that Freemasonry and Catholicism can be mutually reconciled. This is an attempt to open up the Catholic Church to the spirit of Freemasonry. Hence, we have to explain and declare the true spirit of Freemasonry and their aims based on documentary evidence. There's a very good recent book written by the Spanish author Alberto Bárcena, who was previously a Mason. It is called *Iglesia y Masonería: Las dos ciudades*, and documents the spirit, rites, principles, and activities of Freemasonry from their foundation until now. This is a solid and serious study. I would recommend such studies. It would be good to publish a short synthesis about Freemasonry for a general audience.

In legal terms, the Catholic Church is a perfect society (societas perfecta): not a branch of the state, but an entirely independent entity, which has all the necessary resources and conditions to achieve its specific goal.[8] As a result of the Church's own self-definition, the Church has indirect power over the state (subordinatio indirecta).[9] I hope I

---

8   The Magisterium started to use the phrase "perfect society" in the middle of the nineteenth century. It was Pope Pius IX (1846–1878) who first referred to the Church as a perfect society in his apostolic letter *Cum Catholica Ecclesia* in 1860. Protecting the rights of the Church, Pope Pius IX calls the Church a perfect society in *Singulari Quadam* (1854), *Multis Gravibusque* (1860), *Maxima Quidem Laetitia* (1862) and *Vix Dum a Nobis* (1874). Point 19 of the *Syllabus Errorum* (1864) dismisses the notion that the Church is not a perfect society. Pope Leo XIII uses the phrase in his encyclical letters *Diuturnum Illud* on the origin of civil power (1881), *Immortale Dei* on the Christian constitution of states (1885), and *Sapientiae Christianae* on Christians as citizens (1890). The First Vatican Council did not use it, which is, however, probably due to the interruption of the council, as the draft document on the Church included the phrase. Although the term "perfect society" is not contained in the 1917 CIC, it is part of the first sentence of Benedict XV's Apostolic Constitution *Providentissima Mater Ecclesia* introducing the Codex. Through its supreme Magisterium, the Church regularly used the term until the time of Pope Pius XII.
9   Alfredo Ottaviani, *Institutiones iuris publici ecclesiastici*, vol. II (Rome: Typis Polyglottis Vaticanis, 1947), 140.

am not very much mistaken to say that the Church exercises all the legitimate forms of government: its main structure is monarchical and hierarchical, corresponding to the divine order and human nature; it has an aristocracy; it acts as a dictator, if necessary; and — within specific bounds — it is democratic.

The perfect society is the spiritual one, not the temporal. We distinguish between nature and grace. The Church is a supernatural organization. She is a supernatural reality bringing life in Christ and guiding all the people in the body of Christ to their final aim — to heaven, to eternity. I would say that nature itself has a monarchical structure. These are the laws of nature. When you see all the organisms, the living organisms, they are completely hierarchical, in some way monarchically structured. As a qualified biologist, you know it well: nature is organized and structured from high to low. In nature we find a demonstration of the hierarchical and monarchical principle.

Monarchy means that there is a supreme principle or being who rules the others. God, the tripersonal God, is the one who rules all things. Hence, we can see that the entire universe is monarchical, because there is a supreme monarch, the Most Holy Trinity. Only inside the Holy Trinity is there no hierarchy, because the three divine Persons are coequal. Outside of God, all that is created is constituted in a hierarchical and monarchical structure; hence, not in a democratic structure. All spiritual realities are hierarchical: the angels in the order of their choirs, and the Church as well. There is the pope, the bishops, the priests, the lay faithful — all are hierarchically structured, a structure that culminates in the supreme shepherd with universal pastoral authority even over his brothers in the episcopacy. Monarchy means that there is a supreme governor; it is God who is that supreme governor for all of creation.

Thus, we already have a demonstration that the best human form of living together is under a monarchy. Of course, a monarchy can be realized in different forms: parliamentary, constitutional, even with the participation of the people through referendums or consultations. The monarchical principle and structure should, in my opinion, be realized, if possible, in the political organization of a nation.

This should be strongly emphasized again in the social teaching of the Church. Democracy controlled by secular, liberal, and generally secret oligarchies won't work. Truth cannot be subject to majority vote and power relations. A healthy society is hierarchical, deriving both truth and power from Christ and the Church.

Of course. This is the question of the social kingship of Jesus Christ. He must be the king of all societies, even of temporal society. Since ancient times this was always the conviction. It was especially St Augustine and also the other Fathers of the Church who said that the political authority has to recognize Christ as Lord, and follow His rules in the governance and conduct of temporal society. Until the Second Vatican Council, the popes taught the social kingship of Christ very clearly.

Regarding illegal immigration, Your Excellency has noted that there is an "orchestrated plan by international powers to radically change the Christian identity of European populations."[10] *The Prime Minister of Hungary, Viktor Orbán, and the Hungarian government have held this position ever since the migration crisis started (2015). Migration has only increased more and more across the member states of the EU. For us Europeans, this is a real and serious problem. There is every indication that the mistaken interpretation of freedom by the EU, the insanity and recklessness of EU bureaucrats of the Left, as well as organized forces interested in migration are all facilitating Islamic imperialism.*

---

10   Francesco Boezi, "Dietro i migranti c'è un piano per cambiare i popoli europei," *Il Giornale*, June 28, 2018, www.ilgiornale.it/news/cronache/dietro-i-migranti-c-piano-cambiare-i-popoli-europei-1545835.html.

Yes, this is clearly so. There are documents already from the 1950s, from people linked to the United Nations, in which one can read that Europe must acquire a new "shape." A new European man must be created, a mixture of different races. We are now witnessing the gradual realization of this plan. The transportation of people from the Near East and Middle East who are mostly Muslims, and then the transportation of people from Africa by boat, is an operation orchestrated behind the scenes by a powerful political clique of the European Union. The goal is not only to make the European nations disappear, but to create in their place a new pan-European man. More dangerous still is the goal to de-Christianize Europe, especially through the orchestrated immigration of mostly Muslim people to Europe. It is only a question of time before these Islamic families gain the numerical majority among the autochthonous European population, because of their large families and the decline of the birth rate among the European people.[11] It becomes only a question of mathematics that the Islamic population in Europe will be the majority, and the Christians the minority.[12] When Muslims are in the majority and especially when they gain political power, they will spread the Islamic way of life, their Islamic convictions, and impose Sharia law. Subsequently, Catholics and the Christian faith will be marginalized. This, in my opinion, is a plan on the part of powerful political structures that are anti-Christian. They use Muslim migrants as instruments for the de-Christianization of Europe. This is obvious. It would be naïve to deny it.

---

11   The proportion of the Muslim population is expected to rise very quickly in the decades to come: from 4.9% in 2018 to at least 7.4% and as high as 14% by 2050, depending on migration rates. Source: www.pewresearch.org/fact-tank/2017/12/04/europes-muslim-population-will-continue-to-grow-but-how-much-depends-on-migration/ft_17-12-04_muslimpopulation_thesize_1.

12   There are two reasons for the dramatic growth: the average age of Muslims is much lower, so there are many more women of childbearing age among them; and they have significantly larger families.

Christian charity has an order of its own (ordo caritatis): first, I must love myself in a virtuous way; then my dependents (spouse, children); the members of my extended family; friends; Christian brothers and sisters; and my nation. In case of emergency, those in greater need are to be preferred, but only within specific bounds.

Indeed: it is a question of common sense and of natural law. When you are a father and you have a family, and people come to your house, you can receive a certain number of people in order to help them. When a large number of people come, a number that is not proportioned to your family and will damage your children morally and physically, then you must defend your family. This is your first duty. You cannot imprudently welcome foreigners and thereby cause damage to your own children, to your own people. This is a question of natural law, and, one might say, a kind of self-defense from invasions.

I think we should be more aware that as long as we live on earth, we are part of the Church militant (Ecclesia militans). We must be continually struggling against sin and temptation so that we may attain eternal salvation. There is a cruel war between the kingdom of God and the powers of darkness over the salvation of our souls. We must struggle as soldiers of Christ.

The Church is militant by her nature. Jesus Christ came, says the Holy Scripture, to destroy the power and the works of the devil.[13] The entire existence and mission of the Church must also be a fight against the devil, against sins. Therefore, every Christian must always be "in the fight." The Apostle Paul said this to the first Christians! It is especially the sacrament of Confirmation that arms Christian souls with the gifts of the Holy Spirit in order to fight the good fight of Christian life and be a soldier of Christ. We must once again proclaim and emphasize this truth. We should

---

13 See 1 Jn 3:8.

not be naïve and let ourselves be conquered by the spirit of the world, which promotes a false peace and harmony. There is no peace here on earth as long as there is sin, as long as the devil prowls around like a roaring lion.

However, we are witnessing in our time the biggest war that humanity ever had: this is the mass killing of innocent babies in their mothers' wombs. This war became worse with artificial fertilization, where embryos *en masse* are frozen and then destroyed. Yet these embryos are human beings who have immortal souls. This is an unthinkable industry of war.

We must become aware again that the Church is the militant Church.

SANCTE MICHAËL ARCHANGELE,
defende nos in proelio,
contra nequitiam et insidias diaboli esto praesidium.
Imperet illi Deus, supplices deprecamur:
tuque, Princeps militiae caelestis,
Satanam aliosque spiritus malignos,
qui ad perditionem animarum pervagantur in mundo,
divina virtute, in infernum detrude. Amen.

PART 2

Additional Interviews

1

Interview with *Adelante la Fe*[1]
AUGUST 9, 2015

As secretary of the Kazakhstan Bishops' Conference, you took part in the 2005 Synod on the Eucharist. Your presentation centered around your childhood memories of the proper attitude towards Holy Communion, and you gave as an example the case of two priests, blessed Alexiy Saritski, who was martyred, and Fr. Janis Pawlowski. What memories does Your Excellency have of your childhood and of the said priests?

About Blessed Alexiy Saritski I have the witness of my parents who knew him personally. My mother told us often: "My children, I have never seen in my life a priest holier than Father Alexiy." My parents subsequently pointed out his qualities: he was very meek and understanding, but at the same time taught the people without compromising the full truth of God's law. He was dedicated to the salvation of souls up to the limits of his physical strength (sometimes he hadn't eaten all day because he heard confessions continuously). In his homilies Blessed Alexiy often said that we have to conserve purity of heart and fidelity to our Catholic faith. Fr. Janis Pawlowski I knew personally, he was my parish priest in Estonia for four years. It was he who heard my first confession and who gave me First Communion. He celebrated the Holy Mass with such devotion and reverence that it left in my soul a deep unforgettable impression. All his words and gestures radiated holiness.

---

1   First published at *Adelante la Fe* on August 9, 2015, under the title "*Adelante la Fe*'s Exclusive Interview with Monsignor Schneider: Vatican II, Communion in the Hand, Crisis, SSPX." The same text was published simultaneously at *OnePeterFive*.

When I felt for the first time in my soul the attraction to the priesthood, at the age of twelve, the holy face of this priest suddenly appeared in my memory. He really was a man of God. I received the great grace that I was able to meet him again in Riga, Latvia, after not having seen him for 27 years. He was already 86 years old, yet he preserved the same fresh and spiritually radiant face. The three days I spent with him were a kind of spiritual exercises for me! He helped me to put on my liturgical vestments and served me during my Mass with the simplicity and humility of a little altar boy.

In your book Dominus Est, *put out by Libreria Editrice Vaticana in 2008, you reflect on your childhood under Communist persecution and offer some remarks on the history and rite of Holy Communion. How has the practice of receiving Communion in the hand weakened faith in the Real Presence of Our Lord Jesus Christ in the Eucharist?*

When my family left the Soviet Union in 1973 and we said goodbye to Fr. Janis Pawlowski, he gave us this admonition: "When you come to Germany, please don't go to churches where Holy Communion is given in the hand." When we heard these words, we were all deeply shocked; we could not imagine that the Most Blessed Sacrament, the Divine Lord Himself in sacramental form, could be received in such a banal manner. It is now a proven fact that a considerable portion of those who receive Holy Communion habitually in the hand—especially the younger generation that had not known the manner of receiving Communion kneeling and on the tongue—no longer has the full Catholic faith in the Real Presence, because the consecrated host is treated almost in the same manner as the handling of ordinary food. This minimalistic approach has a causal connection with the weakening or even loss of faith in the Real Presence.

On January 15, 2012, Your Excellency participated in the fourth Rencontre pour l'unité catholique in Paris, with a lecture on "The New Evangelization and the Sacred Liturgy." In this important lecture you addressed the "five wounds" in Christ's liturgical mystical body: the priest turned towards the congregation, Holy Communion taken in the hand, the new Offertory prayers, the disappearance of Latin in liturgical celebrations, and the performance of certain ministries, such as those of lector and acolyte, by women. How have these wounds been produced? What would the Church need for these wounds to heal and disappear?

None of these liturgical wounds can even remotely be supported by *Sacrosanctum Concilium*, the Constitution on Sacred Liturgy of the Second Vatican Council. They have been introduced according to a specific agenda of a small group of liturgists who fatally occupied key positions in the Roman Curia in the immediate postconciliar period and who with cunning and trickery presented such radical changes (with the exception of the practice of Communion in the hand) sometimes as the will of the pope and sometimes as an almost unanimous decision of the members of the Consilium or committee in charge of liturgical reform. Such manipulations are documented in, for example, Cardinal Ferdinando Antonelli's *The Development of the Liturgical Reform*[2] and Louis Bouyer's *Memoirs* — two authors who were closely involved in the postconciliar reform and so were witnesses of the above-mentioned manipulations. It is a mysterious permission of God that the good intentions of the Fathers of the Second Vatican Council and their moderate dispositions on liturgical reform fell into the hands of impious and revolutionary ideologues. They brought the sacred liturgy of the Holy Roman Church into a state of captivity, into a kind of liturgical "Avignon exile."

---

2   In fact, the book was compiled by Nicola Giampietro and bears the full title: *The Development of the Liturgical Reform as Seen by Cardinal Ferdinando Antonelli from 1948 to 1970* (Fort Collins, CO: Roman Catholic Books, 2009).

In order to heal these wounds, the following steps should be taken:

1) A thorough study of the history of the liturgy concerning the above-mentioned five liturgical wounds. Such a study will compel people to admit with scientific honesty that these liturgical practices in their concrete modern form never existed in the universal Church; they represent a radical rupture with the perennial law of prayer (*lex orandi*) and therefore also a rupture with Apostolic tradition.

2) A careful study of the text of *Sacrosanctum Concilium* and particularly of the *Acta* of the conciliar discussions on this topic in order to demonstrate the real mind of the Council Fathers (the "*mens patrum*"), with the Encyclical *Mediator Dei* as the principal hermeneutic key of *Sacrosanctum Concilium*.[3]

3) To avoid, if possible, these liturgical practices: Communion in the hand, celebration towards the congregation, total vernacularization, female lectors and acolytes. These four practices are not, in any case, compulsory, although they are often treated as such.

4) Since the modern offertory prayers are, however, prescribed in the missal, the Holy See should be asked to issue a document that will grant to the celebrant freedom of choice between the modern and the traditional offertory prayers during the celebration of the Holy Mass in the ordinary form; the same document of the Holy See could encourage the celebration *ad Dominum* or *ad orientem* and dissuade and restrict the practice of Communion in the hand.

5) To give catechetical and homiletic instructions about the ineffable divine mystery of the Holy Eucharist, about the perennial and unchangeable Catholic theology of the sacred liturgy, about the spiritual meaning of ritual details.

---

3 See Susan Benody, "Footnotes for a Hermeneutic of Continuity: *Sacrosanctum Concilium*'s Vanishing Citations," available at https://archive.ccwatershed.org/media/pdfs/15/06/03/13-43-26_0.pdf. — *Ed.*

6) To organize specific liturgical conferences and talks for seminarians, clergy, and laity in order to showcase perennial liturgical principles and the organic character of the sacred liturgy and also to unmask the modern liturgical myths.

7) To spread more and more the celebration of the liturgy in the ancient form and the central claims of the motu proprio *Summorum Pontificum* of Pope Benedict XVI with its accompanying letter.[4]

In 2014 Libreria Editrice Vaticana published another book by Your Excellency, entitled Corpus Christi: La santa comunione e il rinno-vamento della Chiesa,[5] *where you address once more, and in greater depth, the subject of Holy Communion. The book ends with a reflection worthy of note: the "preferential option for the Poorest, the Most Helpless"—Our Lord Jesus Christ in the Eucharistic species. With so much talk about the "option for the poor," for the weak, why are we not aware of the presence of the Poorest of the poor in the Holy Eucharist?*

The fact that Christ under the Eucharistic species has become today the most weak, vulnerable, defenseless, the most dishonored in the Church, is a clear and sad indicator of the extent to which the love and the integrity of the Catholic faith in the Eucharist and in the Incarnation has waned.

To what extent can we say a Protestant mentality has invaded the Catholic Church?

Indeed, the essence of Protestantism consists in the rejection of the fullness of the truth of the Incarnation with

---

4 *Summorum Pontificum* is an apostolic letter of Pope Benedict XVI, dated July 7, 2007, and released with an explanatory letter. Art. 1 of the motu proprio and the explanatory letter to the bishops leave no room for argument, declaring that the traditional Missal was never abrogated and that no permission was ever needed to use it. "What earlier generations held as sacred, remains sacred and great for us, too, and it cannot be all of a sudden entirely forbidden or even considered harmful."

5 English version: *Corpus Christi: Holy Communion and the Renewal of the Church* (n.p.: Lumen Fidei Press, 2014).

all its implications and consequences: the visibility of the Church, the sacramental life, the concreteness and greatness of the Eucharistic Presence, the incarnational characteristics of the liturgy. The current crisis of the Church manifests itself mainly in these two attitudes: a gnostic spiritualism and a horizontal naturalism. The root of these is anthropocentrism, which is a typical characteristic of Protestantism.

Does Your Excellency think the pre-Vatican II Church was isolated from the real world, full of privileges and closed in on itself? Did Vatican II aim to create a different Church from that received by Tradition?

The period before Vatican II, especially after the Council of Trent, was characterized by an amazingly great and dynamic missionary activity, comparable in its effects to the missionary period after Pentecost. Think, for instance, of the missionary work of St Francis Xavier, and of the Jesuit order as a whole, the admirable missionary work of several religious congregations on the African and Asian continents in the nineteenth and twentieth centuries. Through her missionary work, the Church contributed decisively also to a higher cultural, educational, and hygienic level of life in many nations. In the period before Vatican II the Church made enormous contributions to the natural sciences, even through her priests: Gregor Mendel in genetics and George Lemaitre in astronomy and physics come to mind. For most of the native peoples in America, Africa, and Asia, Catholic missionary priests wrote the first grammar books and devised the alphabets of their languages. The Church made a decisive contribution to the abolition of slavery (beginning with Paul III and Las Casas in the sixteenth century down to Leo XIII and the Catholic Princess Isabel of Brazil in the nineteenth century). With the encyclical *Rerum Novarum*, Leo XIII gave universally recognized norms for the just treatment of workers.

Consequently, the Church before Vatican II was in no way closed in on herself or isolated from the real world. Neither Pope John XXIII nor the vast majority of the Fathers of Vatican II aimed to create a different Church. All the documents and speeches of John XXIII, the preparatory documents or *schemata* of the Council, and the Acts of the Council itself demonstrate this well enough. The true relationship of the Church to the real world or to temporal society has always been realized according to the theological principle *gratia supponit naturam*, that is, grace (the Church) presupposes nature (the world), purifying, elevating, and perfecting it. If the Church no longer or insufficiently influences the world and its realities with supernatural gifts (grace, light of divine truth) and instead deals predominantly with affairs of natural and temporal realities (e.g., social justice, ecology), the Church encloses herself in the temporal and deprives the world of the eternal, of heaven. The fact that the predominant activity of many of the Church's official structures (associations, commissions, etc.) is isolated from the supernatural, from heaven, and is immersed in the temporal and the horizontal, represents the core problem of the Church's current crisis.

How does Your Excellency evaluate Benedict XVI's motu proprio Summorum Pontificum? *Why do you think there are so many obstacles to its implementation?*

The motu proprio *Summorum Pontificum* is an act of the Supreme Magisterium with immense ramifications. It was absolutely necessary. It belongs to the very nature of the Church to hand on to future generations the treasures of the faith (*lex credendi*) and of worship (*lex orandi*) integrally, and without signs of rupture. A noticeable or revolutionary rupture in faith and worship contradicts the organicity of the Church's nature, since the Church is an organic entity (Body of Christ, grapevine, divine garden), not a lifeless machine at the whim of someone's drawing board. The obstacles to the implementation of *Summorum Pontificum* are based on the fact that a considerable part of the clergy has a disturbed relationship with the principle of organic tradition and manifests a spirit of rupture towards the Church's liturgical inheritance. One other reason for their resistance and antipathy towards *Summorum Pontificum* is a lack of self-criticism regarding some obvious defects of the postconciliar liturgical reforms.

Can Your Excellency explain what your feelings are when you offer the Holy Sacrifice of the Mass in the Extraordinary Form?

When I offer the Holy Sacrifice of the Mass in the Extraordinary Form — or, to be more precise, in the Traditional Form — I have the salutary and beneficial awareness and experience that I am not the owner and boss (so to speak) of the sacred rite, but really only the servant, fulfilling the will and the commands of the Church, the Bride of Christ — that I am praying in the spirit and even with the concrete formulas and gestures which belong to the Catholic generations of more than a millennium. One has an awareness of carrying out even in the smallest ritual details something which is not merely human and temporal, but eternal and heavenly; one is celebrating the supreme act of adoration of the ineffable majesty of the Triune God, who mercifully overwhelms us with redeeming graces.

What factors are responsible for the faith crisis in which we are immersed, where some aspects of faith are being called into question by the Church's hierarchy itself, which would have been hitherto inconceivable? Is Catholic identity itself in crisis?

The deepest root of the faith crisis is anthropocentrism and naturalism, which manifest themselves in an attitude of seeing and judging the truth of divine revelation and divine worship predominantly with rationalistic and humanistic criteria and with the criteria of changeable human history. Such an attitude leads to a dogmatic, moral, and liturgical relativism and ultimately to a serious defectiveness of faith, which, ultimately, is not so far away from apostasy and paganism. The words of our divine Savior refer in the first place to all disciples of Christ and especially to the current crisis inside the Church: "When the Son of Man comes, will he find faith on earth?" (Lk 18:8).

Can Your Excellency give some words of encouragement to those priests who, for being faithful to Church Tradition, are isolated and pushed into the background in their dioceses and not given churches where they can offer Holy Mass in the Extraordinary Form, as well as to those faithful who are deprived of the traditional Mass?

I would like to say to these priests, seminarians, young people and families: "It is an honor and a privilege to be faithful to the divine truth and to the spiritual and liturgical traditions of our forefathers and of the saints, and to be marginalized for that reason by those who occupy administrative positions in the Church. Your fidelity and courage constitute the real power in the Church. You are the real ecclesiastical 'periphery,' which renews the Church by God's power. Living the true tradition of dogma, liturgy, and holiness is a manifestation of the democracy of the saints — tradition is the democracy of the saints. With St Athanasius I speak to you these words: Those in the Church who oppose, humiliate, and marginalize you have occupied the churches, while during this time you are on the outside; they have the premises, but you have the Apostolic Faith. They claim that they represent the Church, but in reality, they are the ones who are expelling themselves from it and going astray."

Your Excellency has recently visited the SSPX seminaries in the United States and France. We know they were "discreet" meetings, but can you summarize for us what you saw and talked about with them? What expectations do you have of a coming reconciliation and what would be the main obstacle to it?

The Holy See asked me to visit the two seminaries of the SSPX in order to conduct a discussion on a specific theological topic with a group of theologians of the SSPX and with His Excellency Bishop Fellay. To me, this shows that for the Holy See the SSPX is not a negligible ecclesiastical reality and that it has to be taken seriously. I have a good impression from my visits. I was able to observe a sound theological, spiritual, and human reality in the two seminaries. The *sentire cum ecclesia* of the SSPX is shown by the fact that I was received as an envoy of the Holy See with true respect and cordiality. Furthermore, I was glad to see in the entrance area of both places a photo of Pope Francis, the reigning Pontiff. In the sacristies there were plates with the name of Pope Francis and the local diocesan bishop. I was moved to hear the traditional chant for the pope (*"Oremus pro pontifice nostro Francisco..."*) during the solemn exposition of the Blessed Sacrament. To my knowledge, there are no weighty reasons for continuing to deny the clergy and faithful of the SSPX official canonical recognition; they should be accepted as they are. This was indeed Archbishop Lefebvre's petition to the Holy See: "Accept us as we are."

I believe the issue of Vatican II should not be taken as the *conditio sine qua non*, since it was an assembly with primarily pastoral aims and characteristics. Part of the conciliar statements reflects only its time and possesses a temporary value, as disciplinary and pastoral documents do. When we look at things with the Church's two-millennia-old perspective, we can state that there is, on both sides — the Holy See and the SSPX — an overvaluation and overestimation of a pastoral moment in the Church, namely, Vatican II. When the SSPX believes, worships, and leads a moral life according to what the Supreme Magisterium demanded and recognized, and what was observed universally in the Church for so many centuries, and when the

SSPX recognizes the legitimacy of the pope and the diocesan bishops and prays for them publicly, and recognizes also the validity of the sacraments according to the *editio typica* of the postconciliar liturgical books, this should suffice for a canonical recognition of the SSPX on behalf of the Holy See. Otherwise, the oft-repeated "pastoral and ecumenical openness" in the Church of our days will lose its credibility and history will one day reproach the ecclesiastical authorities of our time for having "laid on the brothers a greater burden than required" (cf. Acts 15:28), which is contrary to the pastoral approach of the Apostles.

2

Interview with Dániel Fülep[1]

MARCH 6, 2016

THE SYNODS ON THE FAMILY[2]

After the Extraordinary Synod[3] many people were frightened or filled with false hopes. Those who waited for a change in the moral doctrine of the Church were probably disappointed by the content of the final Relatio.[4] But wasn't it in fact a controlled experiment to soften basic church doctrine, opening the door to serious abuses and similar attempts in the future? What does Your Excellency think about this with knowledge of the Final Report[5] of the Ordinary Synod?

---

1 Bishop Schneider gave this interview at the John Henry Newman Center of Higher Education in Sümeg, Hungary, 2016, as part of the Regnum Eucharisticum Conference. Translated by Gábor Sallai; footnotes by Dániel Fülep.

2 These questions apply to the Third Extraordinary General Assembly of the Synod of Bishops (Vatican City, October 5–19, 2014) and the Fourteenth Ordinary General Assembly of the Synod of Bishops (Vatican City, October 4–25, 2015). Both were about marriage and family, so they are colloquially referred to as "synods on the family." The Synod of Bishops (*synodus episcoporum*) is an advisory body that assists the Roman Pontiff in carrying out his Petrine ministry. It does not make decisions but advises the pope. It can be ordinary, extraordinary, or special. The documents connected with it: an introduction and outline of the subject for discussion (*Lineamenta*), an outline of topics (*Instrumentum laboris*), the post-discussion report (*Relatio post disceptationem*), and the final document, which can have different names (*Propositiones, Relatio Synodi, Relatio Finalis*), and a message of the Synod aimed at the press (*Messaggio Sinodale*). Following the synod, the pope generally issues a post-synodal apostolic exhortation.

3 Third Extraordinary General Assembly of the Synod of Bishops, Vatican City, October 5–19, 2014.

4 *Relatio Synodi,* Third Extraordinary General Assembly of the Synod of Bishops, Vatican City, October 18, 2014.

5 *Relatio Finalis*, Fourteenth Ordinary General Assembly of the Synod of Bishops, Vatican City, October 24, 2015.

Well, thanks be to God, the final report of the Synod made clear statements on homosexual behavior, which is unacceptable in light of Christian morals, and it also contains good and clear words against gender ideology. Thanks be to God. But as I stated in my analysis of the final report,[6] the section about remarried couples remains ambiguous. Thus, those who promote Communion for the divorced and remarried suddenly declared that the final report represents an open door, even if not directly, to the access of the remarried to the sacraments. The bishops, however, must avoid such ambiguous statements in official documents. Of course, the final report is not a text of the Magisterium, thanks be to God, only a report. Therefore we have to wait and hope that there will be another official text of the Magisterium which will state Catholic doctrine clearly.

In an interview I read, Your Excellency said about the Extraordinary Synod that the final Relatio contains a paragraph with the vote on the issue of Holy Communion for the divorced and remarried. Even though it has not achieved the required two-thirds of the votes, it is worrying and astonishing that an absolute majority of the bishops present voted in favor of Holy Communion for the divorced and remarried, which reflects badly on the spiritual quality of the Catholic episcopacy nowadays. What does Your Excellency think about the poor spiritual quality of the Catholic episcopacy? What are the deep reasons for this?

We have observed for many years that many of the official episcopal conferences predominantly deal with temporal and earthly rather than supernatural and eternal matters, although the latter should be considered the most important in the life of the Church. To save souls and to lead them to Heaven: this is the reason why Christ came to save

---

6   Athanasius Schneider, "A Back Door to a Neo-Mosaic Practice in the Final Report of the Synod," *Rorate Caeli*, November 2, 2015, http://rorate-caeli. blogspot.com/2015/11/rorate-exclusive-bishop-athanasius.html.

us and founded the Church. Therefore the Church has to lead people to Heaven and transmit to them divine truths, supernatural graces and the life of God. This is the main task of the Church. Dealing with temporal affairs is up to the government. So I see here an undue change whereby the task of the government, of civil authority, is taken up by the bishops, the successors of the apostles. Of course, based on her social doctrine, the Church can advise the government so that social life is more aligned with the natural law and divine law. But this is not the Church's *main* task; it is a secondary task. Our crisis is largely due to this: the substitution of secondary tasks for the main one.

The Ordinary Synod[7] issued a Final Report, with some pastoral proposals submitted to the discernment of the pope. Your Excellency wrote[8] that "during the Synod there already appeared those new disciples of Moses and the new Pharisees, who in numbers 84–86 of the Final Report opened a back door to the admittance of the divorced and remarried to Holy Communion.... During the last two Assemblies of the Synod (2014 and 2015) the new disciples of Moses and the new Pharisees masked their practical denial of the indissolubility of marriage and the suspension of the Sixth Commandment with a case-by-case approach ... " Here, too, the method is the typical ambiguous language of modernism. We find some indistinct or equivocal terms — "way of discernment," "accompaniment," "internal forum," "orientations of the bishop," "dialogue with the priest," "greater integration into the life of the Church." It seems that in the Final Report (and mainly paragraphs 85–86) conscience overrules divine law. Wasn't this the very error of Luther? It seems to be related to the Protestant principle of subjective

---

7   Fourteenth Ordinary General Assembly of the Synod of Bishops, Vatican City, October 4–25, 2015, "The Vocation and Mission of the Family in the Church and Contemporary World."

8   "Bishop Athanasius Schneider reaction to Synod: Door to communion for divorced & remarried officially kicked open," *Rorate Caeli*, November 4, 2015, http://rorate-caeli.blogspot.com/2015/11/rorate-exclusive-bishop-athanasius.html.

judgment on matters of faith and discipline and the erroneous theory[9] of "optio fundamentalis."

Although these paragraphs state that the individual judgment of the conscience of these couples must be made according to the doctrine of the Church, there remains a lack of clarity. Those who promote Communion for the divorced and remarried, as for example Cardinal Kasper and his group, state openly that while the doctrine of the Church remains, there is definitely the possibility that the divorced and remarried may receive Communion. Thus, they acknowledge the possibility of a contrast or even a contradiction between doctrine and practice. This is also the typical position of Protestantism. You keep the theory or the doctrine, but the works are not so important and necessary. This is the dangerous principle of salvation by faith alone. And the same paragraphs do not state that cohabitation outside a valid marriage is sinful. This is an objectively grave omission. The final report says indirectly that for the divorced and remarried the culpability of cohabitation could be reduced or even not imputable because of circumstances or the passions they suffer. However, the application of the principle of reduced culpability to cohabitation outside of marriage is completely incorrect, for those who cohabit have the intention to commit sin continuously—it is not some sort of spontaneous immoral act of unpremeditated passion. They should rather form the steady intention to avoid sexual acts outside of marriage. With this sort of "logic" such a reduction of imputability of the sin of cohabitation could also be applied to cohabiting unmarried youths, too. By admitting such a theory, these bishops annul the sixth commandment of God. And if this principle is accepted, none of the sins against the sixth commandment will be considered a sin anymore. In some way this appears to be an attempt to abolish the sixth commandment.

---

9   This theory was condemned by the Magisterium: see John Paul II, Encyclical *Veritatis Splendor*, nos. 65–70.

Your Excellency said about the Final Report of the Ordinary Synod that it "seems to inaugurate a doctrinal and disciplinary cacophony in the Catholic Church, which contradicts the very essence of being Catholic."[10] *Can you explain what you mean?*

Cacophony is the opposite of symphony. Symphony means that all the voices combine to produce harmony, proclaiming the same theme. In cacophony, one or more of the voices seems incorrect. It's against the truth of the melody. So when this Final Report fails to affirm clearly the immorality of cohabitation for divorced people, when it fails to state clearly the conditions established by God for the worthy reception of Holy Communion, others will use this failure to proclaim a lie. Their voice will be against the truth, just like a false voice in music is against the truth of the symphony.

THE SECOND VATICAN COUNCIL

At a theological conference in Rome in December 2010 you proposed the need for "a new Syllabus"[11] *in which papal teaching authority should correct erroneous interpretations of the documents of the Second Vatican Council.*[12] *What do you think nowadays?*

I think that, in our time of confusion, it is absolutely necessary to have such a Syllabus. Syllabus means a list, an enumeration of dangers, confused statements, misinterpretations and so on; an enumeration of the most widespread

---

10   In the interview mentioned two notes above.

11   The Syllabus of Errors (*Syllabus Errorum*) is a document issued by the Holy See under Pope Pius IX on December 8, 1864, the Feast of the Immaculate Conception, on the same day the pope's encyclical *Quanta Cura* was released. It lists the Church's positions on a number of philosophical and political claims, and refers to the Church's teaching on these matters as given in a number of documents previously issued. It was widely interpreted at the time as an attack by the Church on modernity, secularization, and political emancipation.

12   See Athanasius Schneider, "Proposals for a Correct Reading of the Second Vatican Council," December 17, 2010, www.ewtn.com/catholicism/library/proposals-for-a-correct-reading-of-the-second-vatican-council-3837.

and common errors in every area such as dogma, morals, and liturgy. On the other hand, one should also clarify and positively formulate the corresponding truths. It will surely happen because the Church has always issued luminous clarifications, especially after periods of confusion.

"Aggiornamento" was the name given to the pontifical program of John XXIII in a speech on January 25, 1959; it was one of the key words used during the Second Vatican Council. What is the correct interpretation of this phrase?

For Pope John XXIII, *aggiornamento* did not mean changing the truth, but explaining it in a more profound and pedagogical manner so that people can better understand and accept it. The pope stressed that *aggiornamento* means keeping the faith in its entirety. It was after the Council that this word was radically misused to change the faith. It was not the intention of John XXIII.

Another misunderstood phrase is "participatio actuosa," often translated as "active participation." Even according to clerics, it means that preferably everybody should receive a task during liturgy. It's as if this term referred to hustle and bustle or activism. The idea of internal activity doesn't even come up.

The first person to use the expression *participatio actuosa* was Pope Pius X in his famous motu proprio *Tra le Sollecitudini* concerning sacred music. The pope explains that *participatio actuosa* means the faithful must be conscious of the sacred words and rites during the Holy Mass, participating consciously rather than distractedly. Their heart and their mouth have to be in accord with each another. Practically, the same meaning can be found in the document *Sacrosanctum Concilium* of the Second Vatican Council;[13] we cannot

---

13 *Sacrosanctum Concilium*, the Constitution on the Sacred Liturgy, was approved by the assembled bishops with a vote of 2,147 to 4 and promulgated by Pope Paul VI on December 4, 1963.

find there any major reinterpretation of the phrase. And *Sacrosanctum Concilium* teaches that *participatio actuosa* means, in practice, listening, answering, singing, kneeling, and also being silent. It was the first time that the Magisterium had spoken about silence as a form of *participatio actuosa*. So we have to destroy the myths about this expression!

THE CRISIS OF THE CHURCH

Nowadays we have to be aware that there is a deep fault line within the Church. The picture is very complex, but in a nutshell we can say that there is a painful confrontation between modernism and tradition. How can Your Excellency explain this dichotomy in the life of the Church?

We have already been living and experiencing this dichotomy for fifty years since the Council. On the one hand, there are positive signs in the Church. On the other hand, serious errors are spread by some bishops and priests. Such a situation is contrary to the nature of the Church. Jesus Christ commanded the apostles and his successors to keep the treasure of the Catholic faith intact, thus the apostles even died for this faith. Those who have authority in the Church must act against such a situation and correct it.

If we analyze the life of the Church, we see that we are living in an extraordinary time. Apostasy is general, maybe everywhere, and heresies run riot: modernism, antiquarianism, hatred for tradition, etc. Unfortunately, we see the signs of heresy among bishops, too. Some historians say that our crisis recalls that of Arianism. If this comparison is correct, what would you point to as the parallels?

The Arian crisis in the fourth century caused a general confusion in the entire Church. The heresy or the half-truths and ambiguities concerning the divinity of Christ were widespread at that time. There were only a very few bishops who openly opposed this heresy and the ambiguity which was represented by the so-called Semi-Arians. In those days only politically correct clerics were promoted to higher ecclesiastical offices as bishops, because the civil government then supported and promoted the heresy. In a way it is similar to our time. In our time, however, it is not one specific doctrine of faith that is denied, but rather, many of them all at once; there is a general confusion in almost all aspects of Catholic doctrine, morals, and liturgy. In our days, too, most bishops are silent or fearful regarding the defense of the Catholic faith. Yes, there are these parallels.

Some suggest that it would be important for a new dogma to define the term "tradition" and clearly outline the connections of tradition with the papacy, the councils, the Magisterium. This new dogma could defend the tradition against both neo-conciliarism and an incorrect exaltation of papal primacy. What is your opinion about this?

We have a Second Vatican Council document about divine revelation, *Dei Verbum*,[14] and there are some very beautiful statements in it. It says that the Magisterium — this of course includes the pope — is not above the word of God or Tradition but, as a servant of the written and orally transmitted word of God, it is *below* it. One should also stress that the pope, the papacy, is not the owner of tradition or liturgy, but must preserve them as a good gardener. The pope must preserve and defend the tradition as a faithful servant. I think it would be good to deepen the reflection about the relationship between the Magisterium and Tradition.

Today, the Catholic faithful must endure the weakness and the dysfunctions of the Magisterium: in the official Catholic media you can hear, read, or see gross errors and ambiguities. What's more, almost every day we hear heresies from high-ranking priests and even bishops.

---

14 *Dei Verbum*, the Dogmatic Constitution on Divine Revelation, was promulgated during the Second Vatican Council by Pope Paul VI on November 18, 1965, following approval by the assembled bishops in a vote of 2,344 to 6.

A significant portion of official utterances—also from the highest office—is confusing, contradictory, and capable of deceiving many of the faithful. What should Catholics do in these difficult times? How can we remain true to the faith in this situation? What is our duty?

In the history of the Church there have been times of profound crisis in faith and morals. The deepest and most dangerous was undoubtedly the Arian crisis in the fourth century. It was a mortal attack against the mystery of the Most Holy Trinity. In those times it was the simple faithful that preserved the Catholic faith. In analyzing that crisis, John Henry Newman said it was the "*ecclesia docta*" (the faithful who receive instruction from the clergy) rather than the "*ecclesia docens*" (the holders of the ecclesiastical Magisterium) that saved the integrity of the Catholic faith in the fourth century. In times of profound crisis, Divine Providence likes to use the simple and humble ones to demonstrate the indestructibility of His Church.

The following affirmation of St Paul can also be applied to the internal situation of the Church: "God chose that which the world considers foolish to shame the wise; God chose that which the world considers weak to shame the strong" (1 Cor 1:27). When the faithful observe that representatives of the clergy, and even of the high clergy, neglect the Catholic faith and proclaim errors, they should pray for their conversion, they should repair the faults of the clergy through a courageous witness of the faith. Sometimes, the faithful should also advise and correct the clergy, yet always with respect, that is, following the principle of the "*sentire cum ecclesia*," as for example St Catherine of Siena and St Bridget of Sweden did. In the Church we all constitute one body, the Mystical Body of Christ. When the head (the clergy) is weak, the rest of the members should try to strengthen the whole body. Ultimately, the Church is guided by the invisible Head, Our Lord Jesus Christ, and it is animated by its invisible soul, the Holy Spirit. Therefore the Church is indestructible.

A CONFUSING VIDEO MESSAGE

*Pope Francis revealed his prayer intention of interreligious dialogue
for January 2016 in a video message.*[15] *The Holy Father states that
he prays "that sincere dialogue between men and women of different
religions may yield fruits of peace and justice." In the video we see the
Argentine pope with believers of other religions, including Jews, Muslims, and Buddhists, who each profess their faith and together declare
that they believe in love. The pope calls for interreligious dialogue,
noting, "Most of the planet's inhabitants declare themselves believers,"
and therefore, "This should lead to dialogue among religions." "Only
through dialogue," he underscores, "will we be able to eliminate intol-
erance and discrimination." Noting that interreligious dialogue is "a
necessary condition" for world peace," the pope says: "We must not
cease praying for it or collaborating with those who think differently."
He also expresses his hope that his prayer request spreads to all people.
"In this wide range of religions," Pope Francis concludes, "there is only
one certainty we have for all: we are all children of God," and says he
has confidence in our prayers. In the last picture we can see the Little
Jesus among Buddha, the Menorah, and a Muslim prayer chain. If we
believe that Jesus Christ is the only Son of the God, and the Catholic
Church, the acceptance of the faith, and baptism are necessary for
salvation,*[16] *and we know that divine filiation is the fruit of justification,
seeing this video we feel embarrassed . . .*

Unfortunately, these statements of the pope's are highly
confusing and ambiguous. There is confusion because he
is putting on the same plateau the natural level, according
to which all people are creatures of God, and the supernatural level according to which only those who believe
in Christ and receive baptism are children of God. Only
those who believe in Christ are children of God — those
who are born not of flesh or blood, which is the natural
level, but from God through faith in Christ and baptism.

---

15   The video may be viewed at https://thepopevideo.org/interreligious-dialogue/.
16   Cf. Mk 16:16.

This is declared by God Himself in the Gospel of John.[17] The above-mentioned statement of the pope in some way contradicts the word of God itself. And, as St Paul wrote, it is only in Christ[18] and through the Holy Spirit who is poured out in our heart that we can say "Abba, Father." Based on the word of God, it is absolutely clear. Of course, Christ has shed His blood to redeem everybody, every human being. This is objective redemption. And therefore every human being can become a child of God when he subjectively accepts Christ through faith and baptism. We must make these distinctions absolutely clear.

THE NEOCATECHUMENAL WAY AS A PROTESTANT-JEWISH COMMUNITY

While the tradition is persecuted, there are some new modern movements which are strongly supported. One of them is the community of Kiko. What is your opinion about the Neocatechumenal Way?[19]

This is a very complex and sad phenomenon. To speak openly: It is a Trojan horse in the Church. I know them very well because I was an episcopal delegate for them for several years in Kazakhstan, in Karaganda. And I assisted at their Masses and meetings and I read the writings of Kiko, their founder, so I know them well. When I speak openly, without being diplomatic, I have to state: the Neocatechumenate is a Protestant-Jewish[20] community inside the Church, with Catholic decorations only. The most dangerous aspect is their

---

17   Cf. Jn 3:4–6.
18   Cf. Rom 8:15: "For you did not receive a spirit of slavery to fall back into fear, but you received a spirit of adoption, through which we cry, 'Abba, Father!'"
19   The Neocatechumenal Way (Neocatechumenate) is an organization dedicated to the Christian formation of people. It was formed in Madrid in 1964 by Kiko Argüello and Carmen Hernández.
20   The community mixes the liturgy of the Church with Protestant and Jewish elements.

approach to the Eucharist, because the Eucharist is the heart of the Church. When the heart is in a bad way, the whole body is in a bad way. For the Neocatechumenate, the Eucharist is primarily a fraternal banquet. This is a Protestant, a typically Lutheran attitude.[21] They reject the idea and the doctrine of the Eucharist as a true sacrifice. They even hold that the traditional teaching of, and belief in, the Eucharist as a sacrifice is not Christian but pagan.[22] This is completely absurd, this is typically Lutheran, Protestant. During their liturgies of the Eucharist they treat the Most Holy Sacrament in such a banal manner that it sometimes becomes horrible.[23]

---

21   The movement has long sought approval for its liturgical abuses from the Congregation for Divine Worship and the Discipline of the Sacraments. Following consultations with the Congregation, it was the Pontifical Council for the Laity that approved the Catechetical Directory of the Neocatechumenal Way and its extraliturgical practices. Thus, this permission applies only to non-liturgical practices. The decree of January 20, 2012 has nothing to do with the "liturgical innovations" of the Neocatechumenal Way, which should promptly be terminated because they are against the universal rules and practice of the Church.

22   The Council of Trent (1545–1563) declared as a dogma that, as opposed to the Protestant view, the sacrifice of the Holy Mass includes a propitiatory element (DH 1743, 1753). The sacrifice was ordered by Christ himself. It is not only a simple commemoration, glorification, or thanksgiving, but a real propitiatory sacrifice for the living and the dead. The fact that the Mass is a real sacrifice does not mean that Christ's sacrifice on Calvary must be repeated: the Church does not turn Christ's sacrifice into a pagan human sacrifice. Rather, the sacrifice of the Holy Mass makes present in our midst, under sacramental signs, Christ's one and only sacrifice for the salvation of the human race. It is thus a "commemoration" in the sense of a bringing into the present of the reality of the Passion, Death, Resurrection, and Ascension (DH 1740), with Christ as the same high priest in the Mass as on the Cross (DH 1743).

23   The liturgy of the Neocatechumenal Way does not comply with the General Instruction of the Roman Missal or the other liturgical rules but features its own liturgical innovations and abuses. The Vatican has called attention to problems like sermons from laymen in their Mass, the faithful dancing during liturgy and standing rather than kneeling during the Eucharistic prayer, receiving Holy Communion in a sitting posture, and passing a huge chalice with Christ's blood in it from hand to hand. Regulations on church music are completely ignored. Another problem is that the Way separates the faithful from the parish and the church: their Sunday Holy Mass is always

They sit while receiving Holy Communion, and then they lose the fragments because they do not take care of them, and after Communion they dance instead of praying and adoring Jesus in silence. This is really worldly and pagan, naturalistic.

The problem may not be limited to praxis...

The second danger is their ideology. The main idea of the Neocatechumenate according to their founder Kiko Argüello is the following: the Church had an ideal life only until Constantine in the fourth century—only *this* was actually the Church as Christ intended. With Constantine, the Church started to degenerate: doctrinal degeneration, liturgical and moral degeneration.[24] And the Church reached the rock bottom of this degeneration of doctrine and liturgy with the decrees of the Council of Trent! Contrary to his opinion, the opposite is true: Trent was one of the high points of the history of the Church because of the clarity of doctrine and discipline. According to Kiko, the dark age of the Church lasted from the fourth century until the Second Vatican Council. It was only with Vatican II that light flooded back into the Church. This is a heresy, because it amounts to saying that the Holy Spirit had abandoned the Church. And this is sectarian, very much in line with Martin Luther, who said that until him the Church had

---

celebrated Saturday evening as the "private Mass" of the community, usually not in a church but at a profane place, e.g., in a community room, since for them the construction of grand churches is a corruption introduced in the time of Constantine.

24   On June 13, 313, Constantine issued the Edict of Milan, ending the persecution of Christians and acknowledging Christianity as a valid religion of the Roman Empire. In 315, he terminated crucifixion as a form of execution and granted to the Church all the existing privileges of pagan religions. In 321, Constantine declared Sunday a holiday. As an absolute ruler he helped to establish the institutional basis of the Church throughout the Empire from 324 on. The establishment of the institutional structure and the social-political strengthening of the Church as well as the alliance of throne and altar are considered by Protestants as the victory of paganism.

been in darkness and it was only through him that the light of the Gospel returned in the Church. The position of Kiko is fundamentally the same, only he postulates a dark period of the Church lasting from Constantine to Vatican II! In this way they misinterpret the Second Vatican Council. They say that they are the Council's apostles and justify their heretical practices and teachings in its name. This is a grave abuse.

How could this community be officially allowed by the Church?

This is another tragedy. They established a powerful lobby in the Vatican at least thirty years ago. And there is another deception: at their events they present to the bishops many fruits of conversion and many vocations. Bishops are blinded by the fruits, not examining them and not seeing the errors. The members of this movement have large families, they have a lot of children and a high moral standard in family life. This is, of course, a good thing. However, there is also a kind of exaggerated pressure on families to maximize the number of children. And they say, "we accept *Humanae Vitae*,"[25] and this, again, is good. But in the end that too is insufficient, because there are also Protestants with a high moral standard who also have a large number of children and protest against gender ideology and homosexuality. But, for me, that is not a decisive criterion of truth! There are Protestant communities that convert a lot of sinners, people who lived with addictions such as alcoholism and drugs. So the fruit of conversions is not a decisive criterion. I will not invite into my diocese a good Protestant group that converts sinners and has lots of children, and ask them to engage in apostolate! This is the mistake many bishops make who are blinded by the so-called fruits.

---

25   *Humanae Vitae*, an encyclical written by Pope Paul VI and issued on July 25, 1968, reaffirms the orthodox teaching of the Catholic Church regarding married love, openness to life, and the continued rejection of contraception.

What is the cornerstone of doctrine?

The doctrine of the Eucharist. This is the heart. It is an error to look first at the "fruits" and ignore, or fail to take care of, doctrine and liturgy. I am sure that a time will come when the Church will objectively examine this organization in depth, without the pressure of the Neocatechumenal Way's lobbies, and then their errors in doctrine and liturgy will be exposed.

CHRIST IS THE ONLY SAVIOR

Fifty years ago, the declaration Nostra Aetate[26] *of the Second Vatican Council was promulgated. Its fourth article presents the relationship between the Catholic Church and the Jewish people in a new theological framework. This document is one of the most problematic and controversial council documents because, among other things, of its statements about the Jews. And for its semi-centenary, a new document[27] was written by Cardinal Kurt Koch on behalf of the Holy See, where we can read that "the Catholic Church neither conducts nor supports any specific institutional mission work directed towards Jews."[28] Is Jesus' missionary imperative[29] no longer valid?*

---

26   *Nostra Aetate* is the Second Vatican Council's Declaration on the Relation of the Church with Non-Christian Religions. Passed by a vote of 2,221 to 88 of the assembled bishops, this declaration was promulgated by Pope Paul VI on October 28, 1965. The first draft, entitled *Decretum de Iudaeis* (Decree on the Jews), was completed in November 1961, approximately fourteen months after Cardinal Bea was commissioned for the purpose by Pope John XXIII. This draft essentially went nowhere, never having been submitted to the Council, which opened on October 11, 1962.

27   Commission for Religious Relations with the Jews, "The Gifts and the Calling of God are Irrevocable" (Rom 11:29): A Reflection on Theological Questions Pertaining to Catholic-Jewish Relations, on the Occasion of the 50th Anniversary of 'Nostra aetate,'" December 10, 2015, www.vatican.va/roman_curia/pontifical_councils/chrstuni/relations-jews-docs/rc_pc_chrstuni_doc_20151210_ebraismo-nostra-aetate_en.html.

28   Ibid., 40.

29   "Go therefore and make disciples of all nations, baptizing them in the name of the Father, and of the Son, and of the Holy Spirit, teaching them to observe all that I have commanded you" (Mt 28:19–20).

That is impossible because it would be absolutely contrary to the word of Christ. Indeed, Jesus Christ said: "I was sent only to the lost sheep of the house of Israel" (Mt 15:24). His mission continues, he has not abolished it. He said, "go to all nations and make them my disciples"[30]; he did not say "go to all nations — with the exception of the Jews." That is against the will of God and against the entire history of the life of the Church for two thousand years. The Church has always preached to everyone, irrespective of nation and religion. Christ is the one and only Redeemer. Today, the Jews reject the covenant of God, for all covenants culminate in Christ: the Old Covenant was only preparatory and achieved its aim in the New and Everlasting Covenant. That's also the teaching of the Second Vatican Council, by the way: "The principal purpose to which the plan of the old covenant was directed was to prepare for the coming of Christ. God, the inspirer and author of both Testaments, wisely arranged that the New Testament be hidden in the Old and the Old be made manifest in the New."[31] The Jewish people rejected this divine covenant, since Jesus told them: "Whoever hates me also hates my Father" (Jn 15:23). These words of Jesus are still valid for today's Jews: "Heaven and earth will pass away, but my words will not pass away" (Mk 13:31). And Jesus said, If you do not accept me, you cannot go to the Father.[32] When today's Jews reject Christ, they reject the Father and his covenant, too. For there is ultimately one covenant only, not two covenants: the Old passed over to the New Covenant. There is one God, there aren't two gods — a god of the Old Testament, and a god of the New Testament. That is the gnostic heresy. Today's Jews are Talmudist disciples of the Pharisees who rejected

---

30   Cf. Mt 28:19.
31   *Dei Verbum*, nos. 15–16.
32   Cf. Jn 14:6: "Jesus said to him, 'I am the way and the truth, and the life. No one comes to the Father except through me.'"

God in His new and eternal covenant. However, the just Jews in the Old Testament — the prophets, Abraham and Moses — accepted Christ "from afar." Jesus told us this, so we must continue to say it.

While John Paul II called the Jews "elder brothers," Pope Benedict XVI used the phrase "fathers in faith." But the Jews of the Old Testament and the Jews of Talmudic Judaism quite different, aren't they?

Yes, of course. Unfortunately, these expressions of the two popes are to some degree ambiguous. They are not clear. When we say the Jews are our elder brothers, we should clarify that we are referring to the Jews of the Old Testament — the Prophets, Abraham and all the saints of the Old Testament, *they* are our elder brothers because they already accepted Christ, not explicitly but at the level of the prefigurements and symbols. With Abraham there was explicit faith, as Christ Himself said: "Your father Abraham rejoiced at the thought of seeing my day; he saw it and was glad" (Jn 8:56). But how can we say it about today's Jews of the Talmud who reject Christ and have no faith in Christ and the Holy Trinity? How can they be our "elder brothers" if they have no faith in Christ? What are they supposed to teach me? I have faith in Christ and the Holy Trinity. But they reject the Holy Trinity, so they have no faith. Therefore they can never be my elder brothers, or my fathers, in faith.

DIALOGUE WITH ISLAM

Islam is the most commonly practiced religion in Kazakhstan.[33] Traditionally, ethnic Kazakhs are Sunni Muslims. What is your experience of dialogue with them? Islam is said to be similar to Christianity or Judaism because they believe in one God, thus monotheism is supposed

---

33   According to the 2009 Census, 70% of the population is Muslim, 26% Christian, 0.1% Buddhists, 0.2% others (mostly Jews), and 3% irreligious, while 0.5% chose not to answer.

to be the basis of conversation. But is that really so? Is it possible to engage in deep theological dialogue with them? Is Allah the same as the Holy Trinity? Is there any basis of theological dialogue if Islam hates the faith of the Incarnation?

There is some confusion when one says that Jews, Muslims, and Christians follow monotheistic religions. This is quite confusing. Why? Because we Christians always believe not only in "one God," but in the *Triune* God — in God the Most Holy Trinity. We do not believe only in one God in the manner in which every human person by the light of natural reason can discover him. The Jews and the Muslims believe in one God who is one person only. This is heresy, this is not true. God is not one person, God is three persons. And what's more, they have no supernatural faith because they hold that God is one, but this doesn't require faith, it can be attained by natural reason. There is a dogma of faith which states that by the natural light of reason every person can recognize that God is one. Christians have a supernatural faith, and this is an *essential* difference.

Objectively, the God who is known through reason is, of course, the Holy Trinity. But Jews and Muslims do not accept the Holy Trinity. So we cannot pray together because their worship manifests their conviction that there is only one God *in the sense of* one person. But we Christians always adore God in three persons. Always. So we cannot perform the same worship. It wouldn't be true. It would be a contradiction and a lie.

Does that mean that the two World Days of Prayer for Peace in Assisi[34] represented a scandalous contradiction?

---

34   John Paul II organized the first World Day of Prayer for Peace in Assisi, Italy, on October 27, 1986. Altogether there were 160 religious leaders spending the day together, fasting and praying to their God or gods. John Paul II's successor, Benedict XVI, travelled to Assisi on Thursday, October 27, 2011 for an ecumenical discussion to commemorate the 1986 meeting. This time, there was no single interdenominational prayer service, reflecting

Unfortunately, the World Days of Prayer which were held in Assisi contained and manifested a confusion regarding the substantial difference between the prayer of Christians, which is always directed to the Most Holy Trinity, and the prayer of people who recognize God as the Creator by the light of natural reason and worship Him according to natural reason. The most grievous aspect at the interreligious prayer meetings in Assisi was, however, the fact that representatives of polytheistic religions also participated, performing their own worship directed to idols. They practiced idolatry there, which is the greatest sin according to Holy Scripture.

"MIGRATION IS ARTIFICIALLY PLANNED AND PROGRAMMED"

What is your own view about the migration crisis in Europe? What is a good Catholic attitude to it?

This is mostly a political issue. It is not the first task of bishops to make political statements. But as a private person, not as a bishop, I would say that the so-called "migration" is artificially planned and programmed; one can even speak of a kind of invasion. Some global political powers prepared it years ago, creating confusion and wars in the Middle East by "helping" terrorists or not opposing them officially. Thus, in a way, they contributed to this crisis. Transferring such a mass of people, who are predominantly Muslims and belong to a very different culture, to the heart of Europe is problematic. There is a *planned* conflict in Europe and civil and political life is destabilized. By now this must be clear to everyone.

Benedict XVI's view that, while such gatherings may be good, one must not give the impression — even externally, as interpreted by others — that theological differences do not matter, and that all prayer is more or less the same.

THE CHURCH AND RUSSIA

I would like to ask you about Russian Orthodoxy and Russia. You know the Russian Orthodox church, their life and mentality very well. Next year will be the one hundredth anniversary of Fatima. Russia was beyond doubt not consecrated straightforwardly to the Immaculate Heart of Mary and is known not to have converted to God.[35]

We know the text that John Paul II published. It was in some sense a consecration of Russia, but definitely not an explicit one. In the text he spoke of the countries and nations which need this consecration and which Our Lady wanted to be consecrated to her. This was an *allusion* to Fatima, of course; it was an *indirect* consecration of Russia. But it should also be done in an explicit manner, specifically mentioning Russia. I hope that will be done in the future.[36]

Catholic Tradition and the liturgy in the usus antiquior *could help true ecumenism with Orthodoxy. Unfortunately the Orthodox are appalled at the sight of the modern Roman Mass. They say that we are like Protestants. This is tragic if we think about the common Apostolic Tradition found at the root of the Latin and Greek liturgies.*

Of course, that's true. I often have contact with Orthodox clergy and they say the same things to me: celebrating towards the people, the use of women as lectors, the priest and the faithful in a closed circle, the celebration like a meeting and a conference, the informal aspects during Mass — all is more similar to Protestant worship, and against the Catholic and Apostolic tradition that we have in

---

35   See the Congregation for the Doctrine of the Faith, "The Message of Fatima": "The third part of the secret refers to Our Lady's words: 'If not, [Russia] will spread her errors throughout the world, causing wars and persecutions of the Church. The good will be martyred; the Holy Father will have much to suffer; various nations will be annihilated' (July 13, 1917).... 'If my requests are heeded, Russia will be converted, and there will be peace; if not, she will spread her errors throughout the world, etc.'"
36   Pope Francis consecrated Russia — together with Ukraine — to the Immaculate Heart of Mary on March 25, 2022. —*Ed.*

common with the Orthodox. I am convinced that when we
return to the traditional liturgy or at least celebrate the new
order of Mass in a traditional manner, we will draw closer
to our Orthodox brothers, at least on the liturgical level. In
2001, John Paul II gave an address to the Congregation for
Divine Worship in which he included a very interesting
phrase — he spoke expressly about the traditional Roman
liturgy, which is highly venerable and has similarities to the
venerable Eastern liturgies.[37]

*Pope Francis and the Russian Orthodox Patriarch Kirill of Moscow and
All Russia met in Havana, Cuba on February 12, 2016 to sign a historic
joint declaration.[38] This document includes thirty points, with only
three referring to theological questions; the rest refer to world peace,*

---

37   Here are some of John Paul II's remarks on that occasion: "The Sacred
Liturgy, which the Constitution *Sacrosanctum Concilium* considers the summit
of the life of the Church, can never be reduced to a merely aesthetic reality,
neither can it be considered an instrument whose aims are mainly pedagogical or ecumenical. The celebration of the Sacred Mysteries is, first of all, an
act of praise of the Sovereign Majesty of God, Three in One, an expression
willed by God Himself.... The celebration of the Liturgy is an act of the
virtue of religion that, consistent with its nature, must be characterized by a
profound sense of the sacred. In this, man and the entire community must
be aware of being, in a special way, in the presence of Him who is thrice
holy and transcendent. Consequently, the attitude of imploring cannot but be
permeated by reverence and by the sense of awe that comes from knowing that
one is in the presence of the majesty of God. Did God not want to express
this when He ordered Moses to take off his sandals before the burning bush?
Did not the attitude of Moses and Eli who dared not look at God *facie ad
faciem* [face to face] arise from this awareness? The People of God need to see
priests and deacons behave in a way that is full of reverence and dignity, in
order to help them to penetrate invisible things without unnecessary words
or explanations. In the Roman Missal of Saint Pius V, as in several Eastern
liturgies, there are very beautiful prayers through which the priest expresses
the most profound sense of humility and reverence before the Sacred Mysteries: they reveal the very substance of the Liturgy." Address to the Plenary
Assembly of the Congregation for Divine Worship and the Discipline of
the Sacraments, September 21, 2001. Source: *Adoremus*, December 15, 2001,
https://adoremus.org/2001/12/pope-john-paul-ii-addresses-liturgical-assembly/.
38   "Joint Declaration of Pope Francis and Patriarch Kirill," *Vatican Radio*,
February 12, 2016, http://en.radiovaticana.va/news/2016/02/12/joint_decla-
ration_of_pope_francis_and_patriarch_kirill/1208117.

social issues, protection of life, marriage, environmental protection, and religious freedom. What is the significance of this meeting?

The very fact that a Roman Pontiff and a Russian Patriarch met for the first time in history is of special significance. At the human and psychological level such a meeting removed centuries-old mutual mistrust and alienation. So in this sense it was an important meeting. The theological questions, however, were almost totally excluded. The circumstances of the meeting had also a clearly political dimension. We hope that Divine Providence will use this meeting to lead to future unity in the Catholic faith.

WE MUST REPENT OF OUR SINS

Pope Francis opened the Iubilaeum Extraordinarium Misericordiae (Extraordinary Jubilee of Mercy), a period of prayer held from the Feast of the Immaculate Conception (December 8), 2015 to the new-rite Feast of Christ the King (November 20), 2016. We hear a lot of teachings and meditations about mercy. How do you understand the mercy of God?

God's mercy is his love for us. And the mercy of God was revealed to us when he came to us and became one of us. It is the ineffable mercy of God that he decided to become man and redeemed us on the cross. The mercy of God lies in the fact that he is always ready to forgive us when we sincerely repent of our sin. At the time Peter asked Jesus, "When my brother sins against me, shall I forgive him seven times?," Jesus answered: "not seven times but seventy-seven times," that is, every time your brother sincerely asks you for forgiveness. Whenever we ask God to forgive our sins, no matter how great and horrible they are, he will forgive us provided that we repent of them sincerely, that is, we are ready to avoid them in the future. But, unfortunately, the group of Cardinal Kasper and those clerics who support his theory misinterpret and abuse the concept of mercy. They have introduced the possibility that God forgives even when we do not repent and have the firm intention to avoid the sin in the future. Ultimately, this means a complete destruction of the true concept of divine mercy. Such a theory says: you can continue to sin, God is merciful. This is a lie and in a way also a spiritual crime because you are enabling sinners to continue to sin, and consequently to be lost and condemned for all eternity.

What is the connection between God's mercy and the Holy Eucharist? Is the Holy Sacrament the main sign of God's mercy as he gave himself vere, realiter, et substantialiter?[39]

Of course, it is — because the Holy Eucharist is the sacrament of the Cross of Christ, the sacrament of his sacrifice, made present in every Holy Mass. The act of our redemption becomes present, which is the greatest act of God's mercy. So the Eucharist is a demonstration and proclamation of the living mercy of God for us. But the Eucharist contains not only the sacrifice of Christ but also the person of Christ himself. His body and soul are really present, and this is the most sacred and holy reality which we have here on earth. We can approach the Holy One only as a publican who says: "O, my Lord, I'm not worthy, but heal me, purify me!" So the Eucharist is also the demonstration of the mercy of God, which demands that we should be previously purified and washed from our sins. The main and proper sacrament of mercy is, however, the sacrament of penance. The Eucharist is the demonstration of the mercy of God, and it requires necessarily the specific sacrament of mercy — the sacrament of penance — so that the soul may be purified. The gate to mercy is the sacrament of penance: this is the opened gate of the Heart of Jesus. During the sacramental absolution there flows from the Heart of Jesus His precious blood that purifies the sinner. Holy Mass contains in itself the source of all other sacraments and this source is the sacrifice of the Cross.

---

39   Truly, really, and substantially: cf. DH 1637.

THE HOLY SPIRIT IS STRONGER

The motu proprio Summorum Pontificum *will be ten years old next year (2017). Your Excellency has followed the implementation of this papal mandate worldwide. How would you assess the situation?*

As a result of the motu proprio, the traditional liturgy began to spread gradually but very strongly. This movement cannot be stopped anymore. It is already so strong, especially among the younger generations: the youth, seminarians, young families. They want to experience the beauty of the Catholic faith through this liturgy. For me this is a real sign of the work of the Holy Spirit, because it is spreading so naturally and slowly, without the help of the official structures of the Church, without the help of the nomenklatura. Often, this movement faces opposition from the Church's official representatives. Regardless of obstruction on the part of ecclesiastical bureaucracy, the *usus antiquior* is growing and spreading, and to me this is the work of the Holy Spirit. And the Holy Spirit is stronger than bishops and cardinals and some well-established ecclesiastical structures.

"LEX CREDENDI—LEX ORANDI—LEX VIVENDI"

There are some traditionalists who see only the beauty of the liturgy, and they do not care about doctrine. Formalism, ritualism, and perfectionism are very dangerous because these errors separate doctrinal truth, life, and liturgy. How can we avoid these troubles?

There is the basic Catholic principle which says: "Lex orandi, lex credendi." The law of the faith, the Catholic truth, has to be expressed in the law of prayer, in the Church's public worship.[40] The texts and the rites of the liturgy ought

---

40 The axiom *lex orandi, lex credendi* goes back to the time of St. Augustine: if you want to know what the Church believes, you must see how she prays,

to reflect the integrity and beauty of the Catholic faith and divine truths. When we love the beauty of the liturgy — in its traditional form — we should be moved in our soul and in our mind to love Catholic truth more and to live it in our daily Christian life. A true Catholic should love first the integrity of the Faith, and from this love comes the integrity of the liturgy and the integrity of morals. So we could expand the traditional axiom, saying: "Lex orandi, lex credendi, lex vivendi." The care and the defense of the integrity of the Catholic faith must always be done according to the principle "*sentire cum ecclesia*," that is, thinking with the Church.

"NON POSSUMUS!"

During John Paul II's reign, the Congregation for Divine Worship and the Discipline of the Sacraments issued an instruction entitled Redemptionis Sacramentum, *on certain matters to be observed or to be avoided regarding the Most Holy Eucharist.*[41] *This document prescribes that "if any communicant should wish to receive the Sacrament in the hand, in areas where the Bishops' Conference with the recognition of the Apostolic See has given permission, the sacred host is to be administered to him or her. However, special care should be taken to ensure that the host is consumed by the communicant in the presence of the minister, so that no one goes away carrying the Eucharistic species in his hand. If there is a risk of*

---

because her prayer and her belief never contradict one another. Although the principle primarily concerns liturgical prayers, it is applicable to other officially approved prayers, too; therefore, the official prayers of the Church are to be considered as authentic sources of Catholic dogma.

41   This Instruction, prepared by the Congregation for Divine Worship and the Discipline of the Sacraments by mandate of the Supreme Pontiff John Paul II in collaboration with the Congregation for the Doctrine of the Faith, was approved by the same Pontiff on the Solemnity of St. Joseph, March 19, 2004, and he ordered it to be published and to be observed immediately by all concerned.

profanation, then Holy Communion should not be given in the hand to the faithful."[42] *We believe in the doctrine of the Real Presence of the Lord Jesus Christ in the Holy Eucharist. To give the Holy Sacrament in the hand risks dropping small fragments of it and profaning the Sanctissimum.*[43] *From Your Excellency's book, we know that the ancient practice was absolutely different from the current Protestant form. When asked to give Holy Communion in the hand, is "Non possumus" the only adequate answer of priests, deacons, or extraordinary ministers?*

Yes. I completely agree with this. I have nothing to add, because this is so evident. First and foremost, we have to defend Our Lord. It is a matter of fact that during almost every distribution of Holy Communion in the hand there is a real danger of loss of fragments. So we cannot give Holy Communion in the hand. It's too dangerous. We must choose to protect and defend Our Lord. The law of the Church is subordinated to the good of the Church. And in this case the letter of the law—allowing Communion in the hand—is causing great spiritual damage to Holy Church. We cannot follow this law. In practice it can be difficult because in some places people are already accustomed to taking Holy Communion in the hand. However, we should explain to them with much conviction and love how best to receive, and usually the majority will accept it. We have to do our best to achieve this.

What if the superiors don't allow seminarians, acolytes, or extraordinary ministers to "opt out"?

I would prefer not to give Communion in the hand. And if the superior compelled me to do so, I would say: "I can't."

---

42 *Redemptionis Sacramentum*, no. 92.
43 This manner of distribution is a special permission (*indultum*). It is important to note that according to the currently effective rules, the faithful should normally receive Holy Communion kneeling: see *Redemptionis Sacramentum*, no. 90.

I have to tell the superior that I have a conscience, too.

REGNUM EUCHARISTICUM

Over the past few days Your Excellency has had the opportunity to meet Hungarian traditional Catholics and traditional priests in your conferences and Holy Mass. We visited Parliament and prayed in front of the Holy Hungarian Crown and the Holy Right Hand of King St Stephen. What is your impression of the "Regnum Marianum"?[44]

It is such a nice country! I see such beautiful villages and churches everywhere. This trip shows me that this is a Catholic country. And I hope that the Hungarians will be faithful to the Regnum Marianum so that your country can really be ruled by Our Lady. And the reign of Christ is always realized through Mary. So when you are a Regnum Marianum, you should be a Regnum Eucharisticum, too. I sincerely desire that the love, reverence, and defense of our Eucharistic Lord may continue to grow in Hungary.

---

44 *Regnum Marianum* (Mary's Country) is an old Catholic name of Hungary. The name comes from the tradition that the first Hungarian king, Saint Stephen, dying without a heir, offered the Holy Hungarian Crown and the country to the Virgin Mary. Since then the Virgin Mary has been the true Queen of the Hungarian Catholic Kingdom.

3

Interview with Maike Hickson[1]

SEPTEMBER 17, 2017

You have signed, with Professor Josef Seifert (among many others), the Filial Appeal[2] confirming the Church's traditional teaching on marriage. Professor Seifert has now been removed by his Spanish archbishop from his Dietrich von Hildebrand Chair at the International Academy of Philosophy in Granada, Spain—with explicit adverse reference to his critique of certain statements that are contained in Amoris Laetitia.[3] Could we ask you for your response to such a punitive measure, which was justified with the argument that Professor Seifert was undermining the Catholic Church's unity and was confusing the faithful?

Professor Josef Seifert has made a much-needed and very meritorious act in formulating publicly and respectfully critical questions about some obviously ambiguous affirmations in the papal document *Amoris Laetitia*, given that these affirmations are causing moral and disciplinary anarchy in the life of the Church—an anarchy which is before the eyes of all and which no one who still uses his own reason and has true faith and honesty can deny. The punitive action against Professor Seifert by an ecclesiastical office-holder is not only unjust but ultimately represents a flight from truth, the refusal of an objective debate and dialogue, while at the same time the culture of dialogue is proclaimed as a major

---

1   First published at *OnePeterFive* on September 17, 2017, under the title "Bishop Schneider on Prof. Seifert, Cardinal Caffarra, and the Duty to Resist."
2   That is, the Declaration of Fidelity to the Church's Unchangeable Teaching on Marriage and to Her Uninterrupted Discipline, released on August 29, 2016 (see www.filialappeal.org/full/).
3   Maike Hickson, "Spanish Archbishop Fires Professor Seifert for Amoris Laetitia Critique," *OnePeterFive*, September 4, 2017.

priority in the life of the Church in our time. Such clerical behavior against a true Catholic intellectual such as Professor Seifert reminds me of the words with which St Basil the Great described a similar situation in the fourth century, when Arian clerics invaded and occupied the majority of the episcopal sees: "Only one offence is now vigorously punished — an accurate observance of our fathers' traditions. For this cause the pious are driven from their countries and transported into deserts. Religious people keep silence, but every blaspheming tongue is let loose."[4]

When we discuss the unity of the Church, we must ask: What is the basis of this unity? Do we have to sacrifice all reasoned and prudent debate over matters of faith and doctrine — if different and incommensurate teachings arise — in order not to cause a possible rift within the Church?

The basis of the authentic unity of the Church is the truth. The Church is in its very nature "the pillar and foundation of the truth."[5] This principle has been valid ever since the time of the Apostles and it refers to an objective criterion for unity, namely, the "truth of the Gospel."[6] Pope John Paul II said: "Over and above unity in love, unity in truth is always urgent for us."[7] St Irenaeus taught: "The Church believes the truths of the Faith just as if she had but one soul, and one and the same heart, and she proclaims them, and teaches them, and hands them down, with perfect harmony, as if she possessed only one mouth."[8] At the very beginning of the Church God showed us the obligation to defend the truth if it is in danger of being deformed by *any* member of the Church — even when it is the Supreme Pastor

---

4   *Ep.* 243.
5   1 Tim 3:15.
6   Cf. Gal 2:5.
7   Address to the Third General Conference of the Latin American Episcopate, Puebla, January 28, 1979.
8   *Adv. haer.*, I, 10, 2.

of the Church, as was the case with St Peter in Antioch.[9] This principle of fraternal correction inside the Church, even towards the pope, has been valid at all times, and so it should be valid in our times as well. Unfortunately, whoever in our days dares to speak the truth — even when he does it with respect towards the Pastors of the Church — is classified as an enemy of unity, as likewise happened to St Paul, who stated: "I have turned into your enemy simply by saying the truth to you."[10]

Many prelates now remain silent, out of fear of causing a schism in the Church if they were to publicly ask questions or raise objections toward Pope Francis with regard to his teaching on marriage. What would you say to them about their choice of silence?

First of all, we should bear in mind that the pope is the first servant in the Church (*servus servorum*). He is the first who has to obey, in an exemplary manner, all the truths of the unchanging and constant Magisterium, because he is only an administrator, and not an owner, of the Catholic truths that he has received from all his predecessors. The pope must never behave towards the constantly transmitted truths and discipline by referring to them as if he were an absolute monarch, saying "I am the Church" (analogously to the French King Louis XIV's "*L'état c'est moi*"). Pope Benedict XVI has formulated the matter aptly: "The pope is not an absolute monarch whose thoughts and desires are law. On the contrary: the pope's ministry is a guarantee of obedience to Christ and to his Word. He must not proclaim his own ideas, but rather constantly bind himself and the Church to obedience to God's Word, in the face of every attempt to adapt it or water it down, and every form of opportunism."[11] The bishops are not employees of the pope, but divinely-constituted

---

9   See Gal 2:14.
10   Gal 4:16.
11   Homily of May 7, 2005.

colleagues of the pope. Although jurisdictionally subordinated to him, they are still his colleagues and brothers. When the pope is tolerating a wide dissemination of obvious errors of faith and grave abuses of the sacraments (like the admittance of unrepentant adulterers to the sacraments), the bishops should not behave like servile employees wrapping themselves in silence. Such an attitude would demonstrate indifference toward the grave responsibility of the Petrine ministry and would contradict the collegial nature of the episcopacy and authentic love for the Successor of Peter. We should recall the words of St Hilary of Poitiers, which he spoke in a time of general doctrinal confusion in the fourth century: "Today, under the pretext of a piety that is false, under the deceptive appearance of a preaching of the Gospel, some people are trying to deny the Lord Jesus. I speak the truth, so that the cause of the confusion that we are suffering may be known to all. I cannot keep silent."[12]

Let us return to Professor Seifert's own polite critique of Amoris Laetitia. In his new August 2017 article, he raises the question as to whether claiming that sometimes divorced and "remarried" couples might have to maintain sexual relations for the sake of the children of that new bond does not actually lead to the conclusion that there are no moral absolutes anymore; that is to say, that many a mortal sin could, in certain situations, turn out to be no longer sinful in God's eyes. Professor Seifert sees this logic as potentially a "moral atomic bomb" which will lead to moral relativism. Would you agree with him here?

I completely agree with Professor Seifert on this point, and I warmly recommend that others also read his illuminating article, entitled "Does Pure Logic Threaten to Destroy the Entire Moral Doctrine of the Catholic Church?" In his book *Athanasius and the Church of Our Days*, Bishop Rudolf Graber of Regensburg wrote in 1973: "What happened over 1,600 years ago is repeating itself today, but with two or three

12   *Contra Auxentium*, 1, 4.

differences: Alexandria is today the Universal Church, the stability of which is being shaken, and what was undertaken at that time by means of physical force and cruelty is now being transferred to a different level. Exile is replaced by banishment into the silence of being ignored, killing by assassination of character." This description is also applicable to the case of Professor Seifert.

Having yourself grown up in a totalitarian country, what are your thoughts concerning academic freedom in Spain when an internationally renowned professor can be removed from his academic positions merely for having raised serious questions concerning a papal document and for having pointed to the possible dangers of some of its statements?

For decades it became politically correct and "good manners" within the Church to proclaim and to promote the freedom of theological speech, debate, and research, so that freedom of thought and speech became a slogan. At the same time, one can now observe the paradox that this very freedom is denied to those in the Church who in our days respectfully lift their voices in defense of the truth. This bizarre situation reminds me of a famous song which I had to sing in the Communist school in my childhood, and whose wording was as follows: "The Soviet Union is my beloved homeland, and I do not know another country in the world where man can breathe so freely."

Can you tell us any words that Cardinal Carlo Caffarra related to you personally about our current Church crisis—words that might constitute, in part, a kind of legacy?

I spoke only twice with Cardinal Caffarra. Even those short meetings and conversations with Cardinal Caffarra left deep impressions on me. I saw in him a true man of God, a man of faith, of the supernatural perspective. I noticed in him a deep love for the truth. When I spoke with him about the necessity for the bishops to lift their voices in view of the widespread attack against the indissolubility of marriage and the sanctity of the sacramental bonds of marriage, he said: "When we bishops do this, we must fear nobody and nothing, for we have nothing to lose." I once conveyed to a deeply believing and highly intelligent Catholic lady from the United States a phrase used by Cardinal Caffarra, namely, that we bishops have nothing to lose when we speak the truth. To this she then said these unforgettable words: "You *will* lose everything when you will *not* do this."

Do you see it to be justified that other cardinals — such as Cardinal Christoph Schönborn or Cardinal Óscar Rodríguez Maradiaga — rebuked the four cardinals for having published the dubia*?*

The formulation and the publication of the *dubia* on behalf of the four cardinals was a highly meritorious and, in some sense, also an historic act, truly honoring the Sacred College of Cardinals. In the current situation, the indissolubility and the sanctity of sacramental marriage are being undermined and, in practice, denied through the normative admittance of unrepentant adulterers to the sacraments, trivializing and profaning thereby also the sacraments of Marriage, Penance, and the Eucharist. At stake, ultimately, is the validity of the divine commandments and of the entire moral law, as Professor Seifert has rightly stated in his above-mentioned article, for which he was severely punished.

We can compare this situation to a ship in a stormy sea, in which the captain ignores the obvious dangers, while the majority of his officers maintain a studied silence: "All is just fine on the ship!" In such a situation, a small part of the ship's officers may then raise their voices for the sake of the safety of all passengers, and they might be grotesquely as well as unjustly criticized by their colleagues as mutineers or as spoilsports. Even if the captain finds the voices of the few officers at the moment disturbing, he will gratefully recognize their help later when he confronts the danger, looks it in the face, and when he appears before the divine Judge. The passengers, too, and posterity, will be grateful when the danger will have passed. The courageous act and the names of those few officers will be remembered as truly selfless and heroic; but surely not those officers who, out of ignorance or opportunism or servility, wrapped themselves in silence or even absurdly criticized those who took saving action on that sinking ship. This scenario corresponds in some way to the current situation around the *dubia* of the Four Cardinals. One has to recall what St Basil observed during the Arian crisis: "Men in authority are afraid to speak, for those who have reached power by human interest are the slaves of those to whom they owe their advancement. And now the very vindication of orthodoxy is looked upon in some quarters as an opportunity for mutual attack; and men conceal their private ill-will and pretend that their hostility is all for the sake of the truth. All the while unbelievers laugh; men of weak faith are shaken; faith is uncertain; souls are drenched in ignorance, because adulterators of the word imitate the truth. The better ones of the laity shun the churches as schools of impiety and lift their hands in the deserts with sighs and tears to their Lord in heaven. The faith of the Fathers we have received; that faith we know is stamped with the marks of the Apostles; to that faith we assent, as well as to all that was canonically and lawfully promulgated in the past."[13]

Now that there are only two dubia cardinals left—after the death of both Cardinal Carlo Caffarra and Cardinal Joachim Meisner—what are your own hopes with regard to other cardinals who might now step in and fill the void?

I hope and wish that more cardinals, like the officers of that ship in the stormy sea, will now join their voices to the voices of the four cardinals, independently of praise or blame.

---

13   *Ep.* 92, 2.

In general, what should Catholics — laymen and clergy alike — now do if they are being pressured into accepting certain controversial aspects of Amoris Laetitia, *for example with regard to the "remarried" divorcees and their possible access to the Sacraments? What about those priests who refuse to give out Holy Communion to these "remarried" couples? What about the Catholic lay professors who are being threatened with removal from their teaching positions because of their actual or perceived criticism of* Amoris Laetitia? *What can we now do when we are faced, in our consciences, with the alternatives of betraying Our Lord's teaching or showing disobedience toward our superiors?*

When priests and laypeople remain faithful to the unchanging and constant teaching and practice of the entire Church, they are in communion with all the popes, orthodox bishops, and saints of two thousand years, being in a special communion with St John the Baptist, St Thomas More, St John Fisher and with the innumerable abandoned spouses who remained faithful to their marriage vows, accepting a life of continence in order not to offend God. The constant voice with the same sense and meaning (*eodem sensu eademque sententia*) and the corresponding practice of two thousand years are more powerful and surer than the discordant voice and practice of admitting unrepentant adulterers to Holy Communion, even if this practice is promoted by a single pope or some diocesan bishops. In this situation we must follow the Church's constant teaching and practice, for in it we see the true tradition at work, the "democracy of the dead" — the majority voice of those who have gone before us. St Augustine answered the erroneous Donatist practice of rebaptism and reordination by affirming that the constant and unchanging practice of the Church since the times of the Apostles corresponds to the sure judgment of the entire world: "*Securus judicat orbis terrarum*," "the whole world judges right." [14]

---

14   *Contra Parmenianum* III, 24.

In other words, the entire Catholic tradition judges surely and with certainty against a fabricated and short-lived practice which, in an important point, contradicts the Magisterium of all times. Priests who may now be forced by their superiors to give Holy Communion to public and unrepentant adulterers or to other notorious and public sinners should answer with a holy conviction: "Our behavior is the behavior of the entire Catholic world throughout two thousand years... *Securus judicat orbis terrarum!*" John Henry Newman said in the *Apologia Pro Vita Sua*: "The deliberate judgment, in which the whole Church at length rests and acquiesces, is an infallible prescription and a final sentence against such portions of it as protest and secede."[15] In our historical context, those priests and faithful should say to their ecclesiastical superiors and bishops, indeed they may say lovingly and respectfully to the pope himself, what St Paul once said: "For we cannot do anything against the truth, but only for the truth. For we are glad when we are weak and you are strong. Your renewal and restoration is what we pray for."[16]

---

15 *Apologia Pro Vita Sua*, Chapter 3: History of My Religious Opinions from 1839 to 1841.
16 2 Cor 13:8.

4

Interview with *Rorate Caeli*[1]

JANUARY 5, 2018

Your Excellency has been, for many years, a leading figure in the resto-
ration of the traditional liturgy. Now Your Excellency, Archbishop Peta,
and Archbishop Lenga have come out publicly, and forcibly, in defense
of marriage in the aftermath of Amoris Laetitia. *Why did the three*
of you decide now was the time to respond?

After the publication of *Amoris Laetitia*, several bishops and
Bishops' Conferences started to issue "pastoral" norms regarding the so-called "divorced and remarried." One has to say
that, for a Catholic, there is no such thing as divorce because
a valid sacramental bond of a ratified and consummated
marriage is absolutely indissoluble and even the bond of a
natural marriage is per se indissoluble as well. Furthermore,
for a Catholic, there is only one valid marriage while his
legitimate spouse is still alive. Therefore, one cannot speak
of a "remarriage" in this case.

The expression "divorced and remarried" is consequently
deceptive and misleading. Since this expression is commonly
used, we use it only in quotation marks and with the qual-
ification "so-called." The above-mentioned pastoral norms
regarding the so-called "divorced and remarried" — norms
masked with a rhetoric bordering on sophism — ultimately
foresee the admittance of the "divorced and remarried" to
Holy Communion without requiring the indispensable and
divinely established condition that they may not violate

---

1   First published at *Rorate Caeli*, from which the text has subsequently dis-
appeared. It was published at *OnePeterFive* on January 5, 2018, under the title
"Bishop Schneider: 'It is a Kind of Blasphemy' for Sinners to 'Demand Access to
Holy Communion.'" Our text is taken from the latter source, and slightly edited.

their sacred marriage bond through habitual sexual relations with a person who is not their legitimate spouse. In this process of implicit recognition of divorce in the life of the Church, a crisis-point was reached when Pope Francis ordered the publication, in the *Acta Apostolicae Sedis*, of his letter of approval of similar norms issued by the bishops of the Pastoral Region of Buenos Aires.

This act was followed by a declaration that this papal approval would belong to the authentic Magisterium of the Church. In view of such pastoral norms, which contradict Divine Revelation with its absolute disapproval of divorce and which contradict also the teaching and sacramental practice of the infallible Ordinary and Universal Magisterium of the Church, we were forced by our consciences, as successors of the Apostles, to raise our voices and to reiterate the Church's immutable doctrine and practice regarding the indissolubility of sacramental marriage.

Has the Kazakh bishops' conference officially released an interpretation of Amoris Laetitia*? Do they plan to do so, or does this letter mean that the conference believes* Amoris Laetitia *cannot be understood in an orthodox way or in any way compatible with the Catechism and with Scripture and Tradition?*

The text of the "Profession of Truths" is not a document of the Bishops' Conference of Kazakhstan, but a document only of those bishops who signed it. Our Bishops' Conference considered it unnecessary to issue pastoral norms as an interpretation of AL. Even though in our society the plague of divorce is widespread, a consequence of seventy years of Communist materialism, and we do have in our parishes cases of so-called "divorced and remarried," yet the same "divorced and remarried" would not dare to ask to be admitted to Holy Communion, since the awareness and consciousness of sin is, thanks be to God, deeply rooted in souls and even in civil society.

In our country people commit sin as elsewhere, but our people still acknowledge that sin is sin, and hence for such sinners there is hope for conversion and divine mercy. For our people—and even for the so-called "divorced and remarried" among them—it would be a kind of blasphemy to demand access to Holy Communion while continuing to cohabitate with a person who is not their legitimate spouse. Therefore, our Bishops' Conference did not see the necessity to issue norms.

We've had the famous dubia *sent to the pope and a filial correction—mostly by laymen—sent as well. Neither have garnered a response. However, many feel Francis has already responded when he officially endorsed the Buenos Aires bishops' apparently heretical instruction to the divorced, remarried, and still cohabitating. Should we still expect anything more from Francis on this matter?*

The Buenos Aires bishops' instructions do not express directly a heresy. Yet they allow, in individual cases, "divorced and remarried" people to receive Holy Communion in spite of the fact that they do not want to stop sexual relations with their non-conjugal partner. In this case the mentioned pastoral instructions deny in practice, and hence indirectly, the divinely revealed truth of the indissolubility of marriage. The sad reality is that the pope approved these instructions. By this act the pope gave, in my opinion, a direct answer to the first point and indirectly to the four other points of the *dubia*. We can only hope through our appeals, prayers, and sacrifices that Pope Francis would answer in an unequivocal manner the five points of the *dubia* according to the relevant teaching of the infallible Ordinary and Universal Magisterium.

The threat to the faithful has been clear, not only since Amoris Laetitia *was promulgated, but just from the discussions alone at the synods. The confusion it has all caused cannot be questioned. However, much like the usefulness of* Humanae Vitae *was lessened due to how long it*

*took for it to be published, is it now too late to stop the damage, espe-
cially when the pope has officially given permission for some divorced
and remarried to receive Holy Communion?*

We should bear in mind that the Church is not in our
hands, and not even in the hands of the pope, but in the
almighty hands of Christ, and therefore we cannot say that
it is now too late to stop the damage. We can also apply the
following affirmation of St Paul to our situation inside the
Church: "Where sin increased, grace abounded all the more."[2]
God has permitted this extraordinary doctrinal and moral
confusion in the Church with the aim that, after this crisis,
the truth will shine brighter and the Church will become
spiritually more beautiful, especially among married couples,
in families, and in our popes.

*We have heard, for over a year, that a formal correction coming from
the cardinals is imminent, yet nothing has happened. What do you
believe is the holdup?*

Faced with the temporal and partial eclipse of the func-
tion of the Papal Magisterium concerning the defense and
practical enforcement of the indissolubility of marriage, the
members of the episcopal and of the cardinalatial colleges
must assist the pope by means of public professions of the
immutable truths which the Ordinary and Universal Magisterium — that means all the popes and the entire episcopate
across history — have taught concerning the doctrine and the
sacramental practice of marriage.

*If a formal correction were made by a number of cardinals but Francis
continued to officially approve of bishops' conferences allowing Holy
Communion to some divorced and remarried — then what?*

The following principle of traditional Catholic doctrine has
existed since the first centuries: *"Prima sedes a nemine iudicatur,"*
i.e., the first episcopal chair in the Church (the chair of the

---

2   Rom 5:20.

pope) cannot be judged by anybody. When bishops remind the pope respectfully of the immutable truth and discipline of the Church, they don't thereby judge the seat of Peter. Instead, they are behaving as colleagues and brothers of the pope. The attitude of the bishops towards the pope has to be collegial, fraternal — not servile — and always supernaturally respectful, as the Second Vatican Council (especially in the documents *Lumen Gentium* and *Christus Dominus*) stressed. One has to continue to profess the immutable faith and pray still more for the pope and, then, only God can intervene and He will certainly do so.

To the typical Catholic who goes to Mass but maybe doesn't follow the politics of the Church as Rorate readers do — the Catholics who over the past few years have heard the Supreme Pontiff saying numerous confusing things that appear contrary (hopefully) to what they've been taught their entire lives — what does Your Excellency say to them? And how do serious Catholics push back when, at every turn, they're asked by modernists if they think they're "more Catholic than the pope"?

First, these faithful should continue to study the Catechism and especially the great doctrinal documents of the Church — such documents as, e.g., the Decrees of the Council of Trent about the sacraments, the encyclical *Pascendi* of Pius X, *Casti Connubii* of Pius XI, *Humani Generis* of Pius XII, *Humanae Vitae* and *Credo of the People of God* of Paul VI, the encyclical *Veritatis Splendor* and the apostolic exhortation *Familiaris Consortio* of John Paul II. These documents do not reflect the personal and temporary opinions of this or that pope, this or that pastoral synod. Instead, these documents reflect and hand on the infallible Ordinary and Universal Magisterium of the Church.

Second, they have to bear in mind that the pope is not the creator of truth, of the Faith, or of the Church's sacramental discipline. The pope and the entire Magisterium "is not above the Word of God, but serves it, teaching only what has been handed on."[3] The First Vatican Council taught that the ministerial charism of the successors of Peter "does not mean that they might make known some new doctrine, but that, by the assistance of the Holy Spirit, they might religiously guard and faithfully expound the revelation or deposit of faith transmitted by the apostles."[4]

Third, the pope cannot be the focus in a Catholic's daily life of faith. The focal point must instead be Christ. Otherwise, we become victims of an insane pope-centeredness, a kind of papolatry, an attitude that is alien to the tradition of the Apostles, Church Fathers, and the greater tradition of the Church. The so-called "ultramontanism" of the nineteenth and twentieth centuries has reached its peak in our days. To mention just one example: In Rome at the end of the nineteenth century, there was a famous monsignor who led pilgrim groups to the papal audiences. Before he let them enter to see and hear the pope, he said to them: "Listen carefully to the infallible words which will come out of the mouth of the Vicar of Christ!" Surely such an attitude is a pure caricature of the Petrine ministry and contrary to the doctrine of the Church. Nevertheless, even in our days, not a few Catholics, including priests and bishops, show substantially the same oversimplified attitude towards the sacred ministry of the successor of Peter.

The true attitude towards the pope according to Catholic tradition has to be always with sane moderation, with intelligence, with logic, with common sense, with the spirit of faith and of course, also, with heartfelt devotion. Yet there has to be a balanced synthesis of all these characteristics. We hope that the Church, after the current crisis, will reach a more balanced and sane attitude towards the person of the pope and towards his sacred and indispensable ministry in the Church.

3   Vatican II, *Dei Verbum*, no. 10.
4   Vatican I, *Pastor Aeternus*, ch. 4.

5

Interview with
Julian Kwasniewski

SEPTEMBER 21, 2018[1]

Your Excellency, thank you for agreeing to this interview. It is a real privilege to be at this conference and to speak with you. As this particular conference has a Eucharistic theme, I thought that I would start with some questions on the Holy Eucharist. St. Peter Julian Eymard once said, "Let us never forget that an age prospers or dwindles in proportion to its devotion to the Holy Eucharist. This is the measure of its spiritual life and its faith, of its charity and its virtue." How do you think this quotation has been true throughout the history of the Church, and most specifically in our own time of crisis in the Church?

Yes, this quotation of St. Peter Julian Eymard is very apt and true. Devotion to the Holy Eucharist developed in the Church in a deeper and more publicly expressed manner in the second millennium, as we know, and this surely occurred by the guidance of the Holy Spirit, which led the Church to a deeper knowledge of truths about the Holy Eucharist, the heart of her entire life on earth.

As we know, there was a culmination of theology with St. Thomas Aquinas. We have from him and the others of his time the most profound theological and spiritual reflections on the Holy Eucharist. At that time also, God commissioned St. Juliana of Liège to ask for the institution of a special feast of the Holy Eucharist, Corpus Christi. So this was done by the Church in the thirteenth century; veneration and adoration of this central mystery of our faith grew

---

1   First published at *OnePeterFive* on September 21, 2018, under the title "Bishop Schneider on Chastity vs. a Society 'Becoming Ever More Cruel.'"

through exposition and processions. This was not yet the case in the first millennium, but started in the twelfth and thirteenth centuries and developed rapidly. We can observe that the practice of public worship, a deeper worship of the Holy Eucharist, bore many fruits in the Christian life of entire societies.

The crisis of Protestantism precipitated an attack on the Eucharist. In the sixteenth century, the Church restated her teaching on the Eucharist at the Council of Trent. And all the new saints whom God called in the sixteenth century to protect and defend the beauty and integrity of the Catholic Faith against the innovators of Protestantism — they were all "Eucharistic saints." The celebration of the Holy Mass became even more devout and profound around the time of the Council of Trent. There were several saints who started to spread the Forty Hours devotion.

A kind of culmination of this deeper Eucharistic life in the Church was, in my opinion, St. Peter Julian Eymard in the nineteenth century, and other saints of that time who promoted the Eucharistic *cultus*. And so we see that this period, from the Council of Trent onward, shows a deeper theology and worship and liturgy of the Holy Eucharist. We can see that it was one of the Church's most fertile spiritual times: the Eucharistic Age produced great missionary zeal, from Trent to its culmination in the nineteenth century. And the nineteenth century was one of the greatest manifestations of the missionary work of the Church, with the worldwide evangelization of non-Christians and pagans. All this was linked to the Holy Eucharist and to the public demonstration of this *cultus*.

God blessed the people who venerated him. There is a phrase in Thomas Aquinas's hymn for Corpus Christi: "*sic nos tu visita, sicut te colimus.*" It is in the hymn *Sacris Solemniis* in the Office of Corpus Christi. I would translate this, "O Lord, visit us with your graces to the extent that we worship you in the Eucharist." As we worship you, so will you visit us with your graces. And this is true!

Unfortunately, after the last Council, there was really a diminution of the veneration of the Eucharist and public veneration in the Eucharistic liturgy—of the rites, the ceremonies, and also the purity and integrity of the doctrine. To this was linked a diminution, a weakening of missionary zeal and of the fruitfulness of the spiritual life in the common parishes.

However, at the same time, the Holy Spirit awakened, in the midst of the crisis after the Council, a new Eucharistic movement, I would call it. This is the movement of perpetual adoration, which, thanks be to God, for some decades has been growing in the Catholic Church. For example, there are perpetual adoration chapels in parishes, which was not common before the Council. Today it is spreading in parishes. For me this is a sign of slow renewal in the life of the Church. And this movement of perpetual adoration chapels should also have an effect on the manner in which the Holy Mass is celebrated— for the Eucharist and the Holy Sacrifice are inseparable— then on to the spiritual life. This is a sign from the Holy Spirit of the ongoing, gradual renewal of the Church.

How would you say that the Rosary and the Mass complement each other in the spiritual act of being open to the word of God? Mary was open to the Word of God to such an extent that God chose to dwell in her womb—and the Mass is also supposed to bring the Word of God into our hearts, both by Scripture and the Eucharist. So how do the Rosary and the Mass work together?

The Rosary is simply a synthesis of the Gospel. The Rosary is a beautiful synthesis of the entire mystery of the Incarnation, redemption, and work of salvation. And the Holy Mass is the recapitulation of the work of salvation. Why did Christ become incarnate? To offer Himself as the

Lamb of God and to offer Himself on the Cross for the salvation of mankind, and to glorify the Father. This is what it means. When we pray the Rosary, which we can pray even during Mass, we participate actively in the joyful mysteries, centered around the Incarnation; for after all, Holy Mass is a continuation of the coming of Christ in the Incarnation, under the veils of the sacred species of bread and wine. And then the sorrowful mysteries, of course, are a meditation specific to the holy Mass: they help us to contemplate the real presence of the Lamb of Calvary under the sacramental veil. And then the glorious mysteries: Christ present in the holy Host is the Risen, the Glorified, with His luminous wounds.

So, in the prayer of the Rosary we have a beautiful synthesis of the entire Mass. And therefore in ancient times, those who could not read, I mean the peasants and farmers, did participate in the Mass via the Rosary. Oftentimes after the Council, priests ridiculed these people, and humiliated them for praying the Rosary. But this is bad; it is unjust. They participated more deeply by praying the Rosary because its prayers, which are taken from the words of the holy Gospel, helped them to meditate on what is going on at the altar. I do not want to say that we should *only* pray the Rosary during holy Mass, but it is a *possible way* of participating — not the only one, maybe not the main one, but it is legitimate. This I would say for people who have a special affinity for it.

In our times, many religious and laity continue to discover the Roman Rite in its more ancient forms — for example, in the Holy Week and Pentecost ceremonies of the pre-55 missal.

Yes, because, as you mentioned, the old rite of Holy Week, the pre-1955 — already this reform was substantially a revolution, the likes of which had never happened in the entire history of the Church. There had never been a substantial, revolutionary reform. The popes always kept the tradition of the liturgy very carefully. They changed something only when there was a clear abuse or something that had crept in over time that was *in se* not healthy. But there was not a substantial change of the rite itself, never. There could be, sometimes, a shortening where reasonable, but not change; or an addition of something that was meaningful. But it was a small addition, it was not perceived as a revolution or a novelty of substantial value.

Unfortunately, the '55 reform, in its elements and structure, shows revolutionary changes; it resulted in something that cannot be compared with the beautiful rites of the immemorial Holy Week. The changes made were not necessary. What was put in its place was manufactured. This was already an exercise, in advance, of the later postconciliar revolutionary reform of the Order of Mass and of all of the liturgies of the sacraments—of the entire liturgy, even of the breviary.

Along the same lines, do you think there is good reason to re-examine the breviary reform of Pius X?

The reform of the breviary under Pius X, in 1911, was unfortunately also a revolutionary reform. It is an enigma to me how he could do this, because he completely changed the psalm distribution, which the Roman Church had kept almost inviolably since the time of Pope Gregory the Great—even before. So, already from the sixth century, maybe earlier, the Roman Church had, through at least 1,300 years, always kept the order of the distribution of psalms in the breviary during the week. The order of psalms was called the *cursus romanus*. *Cursus* means the course or sequence: the psalms run through the week, from Sunday to Saturday. It was very harmonious, very logical, when you meditate on it. And Pius X completely, radically, changed the entire distribution of psalms. Such a thing had never happened in the Roman Church. This is an enigma. How could he approve such a revolution?

Of course, he had some pastoral motivations about unburdening the secular priests, to lighten their burden. But this could have been done in a way not substantially affecting the order of psalms that the Roman Church had always kept. The problem was Matins, because it had twelve psalms in the weekly office, and for some diocesan priests it was too much. The pope could have avoided touching the *cursus romanus psalmorum* and allowed the diocesan priests to pray maybe only half of them, six for example. So Matins would already be lightened. But the religious priests and the nuns who have to pray as their first duty, they would pray all of it. Unfortunately, the pope changed everything, even for the nuns and for all religious, maybe with the Benedictines as the only exception, who were allowed to keep their traditional psalmody. So I repeat: it would have been sufficient to make a provision specifically for the clergy who are in pastoral work to lighten the burden of praying the number of psalms, without changing substantially the order or structure of the millennium-old Roman liturgy of the Divine Office.

I hope that in the future, the Church will return to the traditional Holy Week, the pre-'55, maybe with some slight modifications that will not touch the substance. And the same with the breviary — to return to the pre-Pius X breviary, which I call "The Breviary of All Ages," with maybe a few reasonable modifications. But I repeat: not touching the substance of it. I emphasize: the Church must do such things very carefully, and she had always done this in the past. The popes have to be conscious that they are not the owners of the liturgy and the rites, but the keepers and the guardians of them. As Pius IX said when he was asked by some bishops to introduce the name of St. Joseph into the Canon of the Mass, he refused, he declined to do this — even though he had a deep devotion to St. Joseph. He answered the bishops: "This I cannot do; I am only the pope." This should be the attitude of the Church towards what is most sacred to us, the holy liturgy. I am not against sound growth in liturgy, but it has to be done very carefully and over a long time, without revolutionary contents or methods.

Your Excellency, your episcopal motto caught my attention because it is somewhat unusual. Unlike most, it is very short and it is also in Greek. Could you explain its particular significance to you?

Yes, when I was appointed bishop, I had to choose a motto . . . and it spontaneously came to me: *Kyrie eleison.* First, I very much like this prayer, *Kyrie eleison,* Lord have mercy. It is a prayer of repentance: we must always have our heart in a penitent attitude, not just when we go to confession. *Cor semper paenitens.* To remind us that we are sinners — this is my first reason.

But the *Kyrie eleison* is an expression not only of a repentant heart but also of trust. Jesus, I trust in you. *Kyrie:* "It is the Lord!" I love the word *Kyrie,* Lord! It expresses all my belief in Him as my Lord and my God, and all my trust in Him. "Lord" is also an expression, in my personal opinion, of love. And for this repentant heart, it is trust, and then also the profession of His divinity and kingship. Jesus is the only King. So when I proclaim this word *Kyrie,* Lord, I proclaim His kingship and His majesty.

And then, *eleison*: have mercy. What every one of us, what the entire world, needs is the mercy of God. This we need. Have mercy on us. It is a prayer of petition, of trust, and so on. Have mercy: *eleison.* This is a very short prayer, and it is a liturgical prayer. It is in Greek, and even so it is in the Latin Mass! It was not translated into the Latin language. It would be "*Domine, miserere*" in Latin. But we celebrate the Mass in Latin with the exception of these words in Greek. The Latin Mass kept still these words in Greek to show the connection with the beginnings of the Roman Church, when, in the first centuries, the liturgy was in Greek. Also it shows the connection with the Sacred Scripture of the New

Testament, which was written in Greek. The first proclamation of the Gospel was made in Greek, officially, and then, of course, in other languages. It also shows the connection between the Latin Church and the Greek Church, that the Church is East and West, that it is one Church. These are the "two lungs" of the Church, the oriental and the occidental, the Latin and Greek. So these were my thoughts and intentions when I chose *Kyrie eleison* as my motto.

You have been outspoken and clear about many issues in the Church today. However, some might say that bishops should stay out of the business of other bishops and dioceses. In your opinion, what is the responsibility of an individual bishop toward the universal Church?

Firstly, I have to say that I have never, in my statements, entered into the concrete issues of a diocese, of a certain bishop. I have never intended to do this, and it should not be done, because that is not my task; it is the task of the pope. So in my statements I have only stated and defended the general truths of the Church; I have only addressed the general crisis, which afflicts almost the entire Church, and the main signs and symptoms of crisis in the entire Church, which are seen in the liturgy, the Eucharist, marriage, the family. So it is not a matter of interfering with any particular diocese.

Every bishop, by his appointment from the pope, becomes also a member of the whole body of the episcopacy. Thus the Second Vatican Council states that every bishop must be aware of and have concern for the state of the faith in the entire Church. He cannot say, "I have jurisdiction here, I have no interest in what is happening in the entire Church. I will be silent, I will say nothing." I think that is not correct. In times of crisis that afflict or affect the greater part of the Church, bishops have to speak up for the sake of the entire Church. This is helpful for the pope, too. Of course, the pope is the supreme pastor of the entire flock of Christ, the Church, and, as having primary responsibility, must defend the faith and strengthen the bishops and priests. But the bishops have to help him in this task by stating the perennial truths of the Church and by expressing desires for healthy reforms.

We are a family, the Church. We are not a business—we are a family. Bishops are responsible for the health of the entire Church, especially in a time of crisis. We are in a crisis. And only a blind person—spiritually blind—could deny that we are experiencing a deep confusion in the Church, doctrinally, liturgically, and morally. Therefore, when bishops raise their voices to defend the truth, they are doing, in my opinion, a good work, helping the pope and their brothers in the episcopacy.

So do you think that episcopal conferences have helped or weakened the witness of the bishops to the Catholic Faith?

It is different in different regions. Usually, in the western parts of the world, the bishops' conference statements, most of the time, weaken the personal responsibility of each bishop. The conference becomes a structure of bureaucracy, and so it can work against the divine structure of the Church. Bishops' conferences are not divine structures; they are merely human structures. It is a collective board, administrative, bureaucratic, which in some way silences, weakens, and paralyzes the voice and activity of each individual bishop, who *by divine institution* is required to teach the truth, and to exercise responsibility as a pastor of his flock. This was clearly, undoubtedly, a negative effect of bishops' conferences in the last fifty years.

Of course, in some countries there have been bishops' conferences that made good contributions to strengthening the faith of the people, with strong statements on relevant issues. But in general, this approach has resulted in a weakening of the divine duty of every bishop to teach, govern, and sanctify. In the future, revision should be made to the statutes of the work and methodology of these episcopal conferences.

In conclusion, Your Excellency, what would you say is the most import-ant element of tradition for Catholic youth to hold on to at this time?

For the Catholic youth, the most important thing is to deepen their faith, the knowledge of their Catholic faith, and the apologetics that they know. The young person has to say: "I know whom I believe," as St. Paul said. They should deepen the knowledge of their faith and also gain tools of apologetics for defending their faith, since we are living in a new pagan society. The entire Western world continuously attacks and mocks our Catholic faith, so young people have to be edu-cated to be courageous witnesses. We should foster in them the spirituality of being soldiers of Christ, men and women who are proud of only one thing: being Catholic. Other kinds of pride are bad; there is only one good pride. This, in my opinion, is the most important thing for lay people.

Then, *not to be conformists* with the lifestyles of this new pagan world. This means to keep and develop the virtue of chastity. This should be concretely practiced by young people today, the virtue of chastity, of purity. This will distinguish us as real Christians from the surrounding, degraded, sexu-alized society and youth. A chaste and pure young man or woman doesn't have to speak much. His or her life already radiates a spiritual power that others perceive instinctively. Young people, with the grace of God, and with the help of good priests, and formation, can foster and develop and pre-serve a chaste form of life. Concretely, this means avoiding all those forms of degradation that are very common, such as pornography, and other things that are not fitting for someone who is a disciple of Christ.

We have to remember: when the pagans persecuted the Christians, in the first centuries, they were astonished at the attitude of Christians. They said, "Look how they love each other." This was not common for the pagans! They were full of hatred; they were cruel. Our current society is also becoming ever more cruel and filled with hatred. So let us lift up the true love, the love known as charity. But in addition, today the new pagans will say: "Look how chaste they are." And just as in those ancient times the mutual love of Christians led many pagans to Christ, today, I think, the chaste life of young Catholics will attract other young people to Christ.

Everything I have described has to be accompanied with prayer. Young people need to exercise the power of personal prayer. These are their weapons. And they should always have one weapon in their pocket: the Rosary. This is the weapon of the young.

6

Interview with Julian Kwasniewski[1]

JULY 12, 2023

Your Excellency, thank you for agreeing to this interview. With continued assaults on the family from every quarter including Rome, I wanted to speak with you regarding the family and its place in the contemporary world. Sometimes there is a controversy among conservative Catholics as to whether or not it is legitimate to continue living in the modern world with a missionary spirit. The alternative frequently proposed is complete withdrawal to a rural setting in order to cultivate the virtues and traditions of the Church. It seems that since God calls individuals to serve him in different ways, both must be acceptable. Yet might there come a time when the modern world has become so corrupted that living in it can no longer be healthy for the majority of Christians? Has such a time come already?

Our Lord sent the Apostles to go to all nations and to preach the Gospel. In those days most of the nations were immersed in a pagan and often immoral public life. St. Paul admonished the first Christians not to withdraw to a rural area, but to give witness in midst of a corrupted world: "Be blameless, and sincere children of God, without reproof, in the midst of a crooked and perverse generation; among whom you shine as lights in the world."[2]

The mission of the Church and of Christendom consists in being, in the words of Our Lord, "the light of the world," and "a city set on a mountain, that cannot be hid."[3] The

---

1 First published at *OnePeterFive* on July 12, 2023, under the title "Bishop Schneider on the Family in the Modern World."

2 Phil. 2:15.

3 Mt. 5:15.

Church's mission consists in conquering the entire world for Christ and establishing His social kingship without fearing the widespread moral corruption of a specific society. The words of the *Letter to Diognetus*, dated to the end of the second century, remain memorable and timely:

> Christians are indistinguishable from other men either by nationality, language or customs. They do not inhabit separate cities of their own, or speak a strange dialect, or follow some outlandish way of life. Their teaching is not based upon reveries inspired by the curiosity of men. Unlike some other people, they champion no purely human doctrine. With regard to dress, food and manner of life in general, they follow the customs of whatever city they happen to be living in, whether it is Greek or foreign. And yet there is something extraordinary about their lives. They live in their own countries as though they were only passing through. They play their full role as citizens, but labor under all the disabilities of aliens. Any country can be their homeland, but for them their homeland, wherever it may be, is a foreign country. Like others, they marry and have children, but they do not expose them. They share their meals, but not their wives. They live in the flesh, but they are not governed by the desires of the flesh. They pass their days upon earth, but they are citizens of heaven. Obedient to the laws, they yet live on a level that transcends the law. Christians love all men, but all men persecute them. Condemned because they are not understood, they are put to death, but raised to life again. They live in poverty, but enrich many; they are totally destitute, but possess an abundance of everything. They suffer dishonor, but that is their glory. They are defamed, but vindicated. A blessing is their answer to abuse, deference their response to insult. For the good they do they receive the punishment of

malefactors, but even then, they rejoice, as though receiving the gift of life. They are attacked by the Jews as aliens, they are persecuted by the Greeks, yet no one can explain the reason for this hatred. To speak in general terms, we may say that the Christian is to the world what the soul is to the body.[4]

Indeed, Catholicism never chose a kind of "Amish method," according to which Amish Christian groups seek to maintain a degree of separation from the non-Amish world.

Do you think that the rapid rise of gender ideology in the past five years has fundamentally changed the climate of secular society to the point that families ought not to expose themselves to situations where this confusion may in turn create confusion in their children? Should Catholics work to have their own "safe spaces" where their peace is not disturbed by such depravity?

Catholic parents must protect their children from moral depravity which in our day has penetrated almost all public and government schools in the Western world. The solution is not to withdraw completely from society, but to create our own "safe spaces," e.g., homeschooling, Catholic private schools, youth associations, systematic training and formation courses or meetings for youth and adults, public marches and pilgrimages.

What is your view of modern technology? Do you think it is a good ascetical and spiritually beneficial practice for Catholics to reduce the use of social media or abandon it altogether? How does one balance "meeting people where they are at" with encouraging more human modes of communication?

The tools of modern technology are not evil in themselves, but they are often abused for evil. Christian virtue consists in making good use of modern technology. In this consists

---

4   Chapter 5.

the cardinal virtue of prudence and, above all, of temperance. It is easier to abandon altogether, for example, the use of a smart phone or of the internet than to use them with the virtue of temperance, which will provide us with supernatural merits. It is important that people should give preference, if they have the choice, to a direct and physical communication rather than using online or "virtual" communication. Catholics must promote the culture of concreteness, visibility, and common sense. Such a Catholic culture reflects the deeper truth of God's Incarnation, the incarnational method.

In your book The Springtime That Never Came *(Sophia, 2022), you speak of avoiding the "mental gymnastics" caused by theological confusion. Do you think that Catholics have a duty to know at least general Church news, even when it can be so discouraging? Or is it fine — commendable, even — to ignore the news on theological and liturgical controversies caused by the current world Synod and similar events?*

Catholics cannot live in a kind of a greenhouse. We must not flee reality, but face reality, however discouraging it may be. Catholics are obliged to know their faith. St. Peter admonishes us: "Be ready always to satisfy everyone that asks you a reason of that hope which is in you. But with modesty and fear, having a good conscience: that whereas they speak evil of you, they may be ashamed who falsely accuse your good conversation in Christ."[5] Certainly, an average Catholic need not know in detail the current theological and ecclesiastical debates. It would be sufficient for him to know the main topics in the current Church debates and events. Indeed, he should exercise restraint in the use of online news portals.

In his book of essays The Liturgy, the Family, and the Crisis of Modernity, *Joseph Shaw speaks of the family as not just a natural institution, but a sacrament as well, and consequently having a unique*

---

5   1 Pet 3:15–16.

and ultimate power in the contemporary conflict. "The effect of the sacrament is to make the natural bonds of marriage unbreakable, to sanctify the natural love of spouses, and to reinforce with divine assistance their natural efforts in raising their children," he writes. These sacramental gifts are not given "to lay associations, to magazines, or even to parishes." Does the Sacrament of Matrimony give couples the unique grace to live in their own time of history? Would it be true to say that this Sacrament might be giving people strength to face evils today that spouses have never had to deal with before?

God elevated natural marriage to a supernatural and sacramental level in order to provide it with a moral power to fulfill its mission in the world. Being a "domestic church," Catholic marriages and families have an inherent mission and power to contribute to a civilization of love. Pope John Paul II, the pope of the family, said:

> The family itself is the great mystery of God. As the "domestic church," it is the bride of Christ. The universal Church, and every particular Church in her, is most immediately revealed as the bride of Christ in the "domestic church" and in its experience of love: conjugal love, paternal and maternal love, fraternal love, the love of a community of persons and of generations... The history of mankind, the history of salvation, passes by way of the family. The family is placed at the center of the great struggle between good and evil, between life and death, between love and all that is opposed to love. To the family is entrusted the task of striving, first and foremost, to unleash the forces of good, the source of which is found in Christ the Redeemer of man. The family will be strong with the strength of God.[6]

A Catholic family will always draw its spiritual power to resist the world's evils and to sanctify earthly realities from

---

6   Letter to Families *Gratissimam Sane*, nos. 19; 23.

the graces of the sacrament of marriage, with the power of the Cross of Christ. Pope John Paul II wrote in this sense:

> May the Lord Jesus repeat these truths to us with the power and the wisdom of the Cross, so that humanity will not yield to the temptation of the "father of lies" (Jn 8:44), who constantly seeks to draw people to broad and easy ways, ways apparently smooth and pleasant, but in reality, full of snares and dangers. May we always be enabled to follow the One who is "the way, and the truth, and the life" (Jn 14:6).[7]

Recently, several authors have addressed the idea of patriarchy and male headship, trying to promote a return to a correct understanding of the role of the sexes. Yet "male headship" can often be explained simplistically in traditionalist circles, and many women who desire true femininity and family feel demeaned by claims which seem to treat them as less rational or less capable than men. How can a restoration of a conception of patriarchy as something which ennobles, protects, and serves women be accomplished?

The true concept of patriarchy is the Catholic one, not the pagan or worldly one. The male headship in marriage and family is based on the order of creation. Through original sin the order of creation was deeply wounded and with it also male headship in marriage and family, infecting it with the egocentric and proud vice of the lust for power. Through the graces of the redemption, and especially the sacrament of marriage, Christ heals this wound in the soul of a man, and his headship in marriage and the family can become like the fatherhood of God and the redemptive love of Christ the Savior.

The teaching of St. Paul is in this regard a luminous guide and a constant appeal to each husband and father: "Men ought to love their wives as their own bodies. He that

---

7   Letter to Families *Gratissimam Sane*, no. 23.

loves his wife, loves himself. For no man ever hates his own flesh; but nourishes and cherishes it, as also Christ does the church."[8] A wife whose husband truly loves and respects her will never feel demeaned by the headship of her husband. He is the head, but she is the heart. Both depend complementarily on each other. Where there is the heartless power of the head, there is tyranny and spiritual coldness. Where there is the irrational power of the heart, there is disorder and spiritual unsteadiness.

The growth of the Latin Mass is closely connected with the most flourishing Catholic communities, with many young and growing families. How do you see the traditional rites as helping us understand the nature of men and women, and their place in society and the family?

The traditional Latin Mass conveys in a marvelous manner the values of a supernatural, sublime, hierarchically structured and beautifully ordered world. Such values attract each human person already on the natural level, since the phenomena of nature radiates hierarchical order and a serene beauty, to which even an unbelieving person is spontaneously attracted. This fact applies even more to a Christian soul, who knows the Catholic faith and nurtures the sense of religious awe. The one who believes in a truly Catholic manner is always imbued with the sense of filial love, inseparably united with a filial fear and reverence of God. The traditional Latin Mass shows unambiguously the beauty of the complementary roles of both sexes in public divine worship. The exclusively male ministers in the sanctuary represent Christ the Bridegroom and with the minutely established ritual they resemble a troop in order. The women have their place in the nave of the church with their heads covered with a veil like Our Lady and all the saintly women in Holy Scripture and the great women saints of the Church. All this helps

8   Eph 5:28–29.

a family very much to live daily the advantageousness and beauty of the divinely established order.

Do you see the actions of Pope Francis in attempting to restrict the Vetus Ordo, and his seeming acceptance and promotion of a non-traditional theology of marriage and sexuality, as an attack on "true love" rather than an encouragement of it?

Unfortunately, this is so. It is first an attack on the principle of tradition, of sacred tradition. Behind this attack there is basically hiding a rejection of the principle of the immutability of the natural order and of divinely revealed truths. And since the Old Mass represents and adamantly proclaims the principle of immutability, it became the object of hatred and persecution, because it is a living rebuke to those in the Church who promote a non-traditional theology and morals.

Clerical critics of the Old Mass often say that it "gives the priest too much importance" or does not allow him to "take his place in the assembly of the people of God where all are equal." How has your celebration of the Old Mass—and pontifical liturgies in particular—influenced your view of such statements? How does a healthy Catholic culture integrate the lay and clerical families?

The contrary is true. The Old Mass protects the celebrating priest from the possibility of being a showman, since its strict ritual rules do not give any space to the celebrant to present to the faithful a display of freely invented words or gestures. A faithful exterior and interior celebration of the traditional rite of the Mass leaves one with the salutary impression that the celebrant, being a participant of the ministerial priesthood of Christ, is only a servant, a servant of Christ, Who is always the main celebrant. The lay faithful have their own specific role in the traditional Mass, which expresses very clearly the truth of the common priesthood of Christ. They are therefore in the nave and follow, especially in their heart, the exterior rites performed by Christ the Head through His ministers. This reflects more beautifully the harmony of the Mystical Body of Christ, characterized by hierarchy, order, and peace, as St. Paul said: "For God is not a God of confusion but of peace."[9]

In closing, perhaps you could say a few words about the books you have published over the past few years: The Springtime That Never Came *(Sophia, 2022),* The Catholic Mass *(Sophia, 2022), and* Christus Vincit *(Angelico, 2019). Which of these is your personal favorite? Which would you recommend to someone first?*

I would recommend *Christus Vincit* for those who want an overview of the current spiritual diseases within the Church and secular society, indicating the roots of these diseases and providing some proposals for their cure and a hopeful future for the Church. I would also recommend the book *The Catholic Mass*, where I show the amazing theological, spiritual, and ritual beauty of the Mass—particularly of the traditional Mass—and argue for the centrality of God while presenting concrete steps for healing the deepest liturgical wound within the Church in our day, namely, anthropocentrism. There will be no true reform of the Church unless the centrality of God is restored in the liturgy. Cardinal Joseph Ratzinger wisely and aptly affirmed: "The Church's existence lives from proper celebration of the liturgy and the Church is in danger when the primacy of God no longer appears in the liturgy nor consequently in life,"[10] and "The Church stands or falls with the Liturgy. The celebration of the sacred liturgy is at the center of any renewal of the Church."[11]

---

9   1 Cor 14:33.

10 Foreword for the Russian edition of his book *Theology of the Liturgy.*

11 "Reflections on the Liturgical Reform" in *Looking Again at the Question of the Liturgy with Cardinal Ratzinger*, ed. Alcuin Reid (Farnborough: Saint Michael's Abbey Press, 2003), 141.

Made in United States
Orlando, FL
02 July 2024

48531928R00093